From Sh-t on my
Boots to Carnegie Hall

D1365310

	DATE DUE		
OC 1 0 17			

From Sh-t on my Boots to Carnegie Hall

A MEMOIR OF A PENNSYLVANIA MENNONITE FARM BOY'S PERSONAL, SPIRITUAL, AND MUSICAL JOURNEY

Dr. Carroll J. Lehman

ISBN: 1533680035
ISBN 13: 9781533680037

Dedication

First, I dedicate this book to my late parents, conservative Mennonites, who nurtured my musical talent from the beginning, for their love and support of me on my journey while they were alive, even though they didn't always understand it.

To my two wonderful children, Scott and Regina, for whom this project was initiated as a jotting down, for them, of my life's journey. They traveled with me for much of this journey with love and respect, for which I will be forever grateful.

To my dear wife, Marcia, truly my love, friend and companion, who has listened to most of these stories numerous times.

To the many people who crossed my journey and guided me to become a better person, personally, spiritually and musically.

THANKS

To Marcia and my sister, Alta, who ardently edited my final copies

To Nancy Robinson who edited my beginning crude manuscript and made great, succinct suggestions of style and format.

The Road Not Taken
Robert Frost

Two roads diverged in a yellow wood,
And sorry I could not travel both
And be one traveler, long I stood
And looked down one as far as I could
To where it bent in the undergrowth;
Then took the other, as just as fair,
And having perhaps the better claim,
Because it was grassy and wanted wear;
Though as for that the passing there
Had worn them really about the same,

And both that morning equally lay
In leaves no step had trodden black.
Oh, I kept the first for another day!
Yet knowing how way leads on to way,
I doubted if I should ever come back.

I shall be telling this with a sigh
Somewhere ages and ages hence:
Two roads diverged in a wood, and I—
I took the one less traveled by,
And that has made all the difference.

FARM BOY

CARNEGIE HALL

LEHMAN GRANDPARENTS   SHANK GRANDPARENTS

MY PARENTS   MY HIGH SCHOOL
GRADUATION

DADDY'S STORE TRUCKS – Notice the live chickens under the second truck

I'M THE ONE IN THE MIDDLE

MY FIRST REAL JOB

COSI FAN TUTTE

AT THE GREAT WALL

MEETING THE POPE

Table of Contents

Beginnings 1942 – 1948 Marion

I WAS BORN, AT HOME, on May 29, 1942 to humble Mennonite parents, Andrew Hege Lehman and Anna Lois Shank Lehman, in Marion, Pennsylvania. Mother bore me in a little white clapboard two-story house that sat on the corner of two intersecting streets. A somewhat broken, concrete sidewalk ran in front of the typical Pennsylvania porch from where many lazy times were spent, watching the little activity of the street. The street was lined with elm trees, old and spread so as to feel like a tunnel as you walked through. Fond memories flood my brain of many trips up and down that street, pulling our little red wagon collecting chestnuts, walnuts, leaves, and in the year of the locusts, hundreds of empty shells. Four tall pines bordered the west side of the house. A sidewalk divided the large garden, behind the house, extending to the one-car garage and small chicken house.

My parents had two boys, Wilmer and Nelson, so Mom wanted a girl. She was going to name her Carol. She liked that name because one of her favorite Mennonite writers was Christmas Carol Kauffman and that some of her favorite music were Christmas carols. When I popped out as a boy, she was disappointed, but the doctor told her that he knew of a male spelling, Carroll, thus my name. When I began school, I became accustomed to being looked for among the girls with the first roll call. I still get mail for Mrs. Lehman and the teller asks if my wife is in the car when I try to make transactions at the bank. I was very happy when Carroll O'Connor became famous as Archie in

"All in the Family". Around the same time, there was a very talented football player for the Green Bay Packers named Carroll Dale.

I was the "baby" boy for six years before my sister came along. For a number of reasons—most of them were health reasons—Mom adhered to the belief that I was something special and the God had a plan for me. The first event was chicken pox, which developed into an infection that created boils all over my body. Mom often recited that she carried me around on a pillow so as not to burst them.

My roots go back many generations, from Germany and Switzerland. My ancestors, maternal and paternal, immigrated to the American continent in the 1700s. I never knew my Lehman grandparents, but they were farmers and plain Mennonites and spoke both Pennsylvania Dutch and English. They had ten children, of which my father was the next to youngest. Many of my father's generation had large families, giving me fifty-four cousins.

On the maternal side of the family were the Shanks. My blood Grandma Shank died in 1945. The Grandma I remember was Grandma Anna, as we called her, forty five years younger than Grandpa, when they were married in 1951, amidst many rumors and much gossip. His children, particularly my mother who idolized her real mother, were appalled since Anna was younger than Mom. By Mother's stories, I sensed Grandma Anna, who was a strong willed, very outgoing, independent woman, unlike many Mennonite wives, was almost the antithesis of my real Grandma. Grandma Anna, however, was great to us grandchildren—loved us as her own. She was a schoolteacher in a one-room school on South Mountain, about a twenty minute drive. It was a great treat when she took me there for a day's visit. The old creaky floorboards and the wood stove blazing left a memorable impression on me. She was strict, but kind and caring. As the years rolled by she became an integral part of my life.

Grandpa was ordained to the Mennonite ministry in 1921 to establish a mission church in Pond Bank, PA. Mennonite minsters weren't paid then, so he had to make a living in some other work to support his seven children. He trained to be a teacher and began to teach in the one room schoolhouse. Occasionally, the congregation took up an "offering"—passing the plate for money among the people in the pew—to give to the minister. Mother told stories of people bringing chickens, eggs and/or meat for their family. To supplement that income to support seven children, he sold various house products door to door—Edjol and Watkins--products such as, toiletries, brushes, soaps, ointments, natural cures, etc.

I attended my first year of school at the little two-story public elementary school, in Marion, just across a small field and cemetery from our house. The ground floor room housed the first through fourth grades. The second story held the fifth through the eighth grades. It was a typical Pennsylvania brick building with a porch. The floors were crude wood planks, the wall and windows dusty. I was well prepared for that first year. Mom had schooled me well in the basics, usually while she ironed. It gave me something to do and I enjoyed it. She taught me the "times tables", the alphabet, simple arithmetical problems, and how to read. Comparatively, I did so well that first year, that they thought I was very smart. At recess, we would be given a small glass bottle of chocolate milk. I can still smell and taste it—it was the best. We had a great time at recess and even though I was deemed very smart, I don't remember much about the academics. Miss Hege, the teacher, was very sweet, kind, patient and caring.

In the summer, the whole family spent much of the time picking and canning fruits and vegetables. We children were expected to join in on the preparation--cutting the corn off the ears, peeling the peaches, shelling peas, or snapping beans on the back porch. Often Aunt Eunice, who lived nearby, came to help, and maybe some of the other neighbors.

In those days, there were many "hobos" roaming the country. After World War II, numerous men who could not find a job traveled the road, stopping at homes for food and often slept under the stars.. Some of them were known to jump a train for long distance stretches. Several times, one of them came to the screened-in-porch door where we were preparing garden vegetables for canning, and asked for food. Mom, always the servant, would oblige and give them some snacks or even cook a small meal for them. I imagined what their life stories were and what adventures they experienced on the road. Even at the age of four or five, our family life and experiences seemed so conventional and predictable.

My father worked for his brother, David, driving a "store truck" for 24 years. Daddy worked hard to give us a reasonable living. He had five different routes for the week—one for every day except Wednesday, his day off—and of course Sunday. Some of his circuitous routes covered many miles before he returned to the home warehouse. Most of his customers were farmers in rural areas that didn't have easy access to a grocery store, who needed staples beyond what they could raise.

You wouldn't believe how many grocery items could be stacked into that bus-like vehicle. There were bins opening at the top for bags of flour and sugar, shelves for canned food and condiments. Deep, open shelves held fresh fruits and vegetables; an icebox and, later, a refrigerator held the perishable things, meats, milk, and eggs. The driver's seat was in a little nook on the left front side. Across from it was the slicer for slicing lunchmeat and some kinds of cheese. Sometimes there was a big wheel of cheddar cheese that was custom cut in wedges, to the costumer's size, by a big, sharp knife. In pictures of the early trucks, you can see crates of live chickens hung under the truck bed. Later, that was the place for crates of soda or "pop".

My father was ordained Deacon of the Pond Bank Mennonite Church in 1941. A Deacon assisted the minister in many ways. He visited the sick, helped with administration of the church and aided in baptisms and communion. The church was our life, not just our religious life but, our entire social life. I don't remember having many family friends in Marion. We traveled to Pond Bank, from Marion every Sunday morning for church services, sometimes staying at Grandpa's house until the evening service, and sometimes making two trips. Wednesday nights we went to the weekly prayer meeting. The trip to Pond Bank was an adventure in our 1934 Chevy. The trip was twelve miles over old winding, hilly roads.

On the return trip, on Sunday mornings, Mom read to us, from church papers that we received at the service—The Words of Cheer and the Youth Christian Companion (YCC). The YCC contained a serial story with a much-anticipated new segment each week. I was the smallest of us boys, so I stood in the middle, between the front and back seats, over the hump, so

I could hear better—no seatbelts, of course. Once in a while, Daddy would allow one of us to sit on his lap and steer the car -- no laws about that either.

I have little recollection of music in my life in these early years, except for hymn singing in church and our Victrola. It was one of those that had a high cabinet with a place for records. The turntable that played the only records at that time—78s--was nestled in the very top. You had to crank it up to make it play.

Childhood 1948 - 1958 Pond Bank

∾

My parents took their responsibilities as Deacon and Deacon's wife very seriously; they believed God called them. The many trips to Pond Bank and the inability to visit sick people, to witness to people, and to effectively aid in administration of the Church, led to their decision to move to Pond Bank. Being very young then, I don't know how it all unfolded, but they bought my Grandpa's small farm of 56 acres—the same farm where my mother grew up. Grandpa bought the property adjacent to this farm.

Several structures existed on our property: an old brick farmhouse, painted white, a wagon shed, that would hold all sorts of farm implements, an old barn, a one-car garage and an "two-holer" outhouse. A fairly busy road separated the house from the rest of the buildings.

The farmhouse was two stories. It had a half porch on the front and a full porch on the side. A large cistern dwelt under the front porch. There were three bedrooms upstairs and a bath, no shower in those days. My brothers and I shared a large bedroom over the kitchen. Nelson and I occupied one bed and Wilmer another. Almost every night, a struggle occurred between Nelson and me over who was on whose side. These rooms were an add-on and open on three sides, therefore quite cold in the winter. There was no heat in our bedroom, just a register from the kitchen below. We would crowd around it when our aunt and uncle stopped in after prayer meeting. It gave us, probably an unwarranted, insight into the politics of the church. An old, smelly kerosene heater supplemented the heat, but it was still cold in the mornings, so we would grab our clothes and speed to the bathroom, which had heat.

The oil furnace heated the kitchen, but a wonderful old wood burning range was there to conserve fuel oil. Dried corncobs made excellent kindling, and we had a lot of wood on the property. A gas stove was used for the main cooking, but I do remember Mom, occasionally, baking in the oven of the wood stove

The barn was an old dilapidated structure, probably built in the late nineteen century. Many of the siding planks were loose and about to fall. The first floor held the cow stable—where the cows were tied up in stanchions for hand milking--with a trough to catch the manure. It held the pigpen and another stable, which generally housed a calf or two, or, maybe, a couple of steers. The second floor of the wreck of a barn held two haymows for hay and/or straw with a space between them, where the tractor and wagon entered to transfer the hay or straw into the mows.

A built-up ground ramp called the "barn bridge" provided access to that floor for vehicles. The span between the two mows was bridged by a couple of very large wooden beams, two feet in diameter. They could be reached from each mow by a crudely carved wooden ladder. Climbing up to them and lying down on them gave us kids a great view of that floor.

It was a cultural shock to move from the quaint, lazy town of Marion to Pond Bank, a typical tough Appalachian town with all the problems of race, poverty, alcoholism, teen pregnancies, family rivalries, and crime. Ore and coal were mined there in the early 20th century, but the mines were abandoned, leaving big craters to become dirty, muddy ponds. The small mountain, South Mountain, contained huge deposits of sand, called "sand banks" which led to huge excavations of sand, thus the name Pond Bank.

Many dirty beat up trailers, small houses, built crudely and covered by asbestos tiles filled the town. We were always considered outsiders by religion, by class, by our "affluence" by the townsfolk. Although we were not wealthy, with hard work and frugality, we had a good living. My parents were careful that we didn't become too close to our peers in the town for fear of "bad influences".

Although we children had some friends in Pond Bank, our "real" friends were Mennonite cousins and friends from the church. We would often go home with one of them on Sundays after morning church and come back with them for evening church or vice versa.

I did have a good Pond Bank friend, a nice soft spoken guy who loved pigeons and we spent many hours, in our barn, trying to catch their young—squabs—from their nests, which he housed in a wire cage and raised. His mother and the two daughters "were born again" and joined the church. The father drank a great deal, had a bit of a gruff character, but was employed and a decent person.

People looked upon my parents as trustworthy, upstanding folks, someone they could count on for aid with many problems. When a family had no money for groceries because the husband spent it all on alcohol at a bar on the way home after receiving his paycheck, my father, numerous times, drove to the factory to bring him directly home.

The stories of the Hatfields and the McCoys had nothing on Pond Bank. We had the various families who had difficulty keeping peace between them. Colorful characters filled the little village. A neighbor lady sat on her porch swing of their log house almost every evening, in the summer and loved to tease and flirt with me, as I walked by—embarrassing me as a preteenager.

The people that lived next to us, first in an old trailer and then a small house they built, were very poor, even though he had a quite good factory job. The mother was a very short, homely woman, who was afflicted with some ailment, often something grotesque on her skin, probably, coming from the filth that they lived in. When she was so sick that she couldn't get out of bed for weeks on end, Mom would take her food and try to clean her bedding and some of the house. A stench, that usually filled the house, was so foul it caused Mom to wear a handkerchief around her nose and mouth. I tried to help a few times, but just couldn't get past that awful odor. They had three sons, one almost blind, and a blind daughter. The oldest one never held a steady job, but walked the roads, sometimes the entire way, about 8 miles, to Chambersburg. The youngest and I became tepid friends, but my parents were confident that he stole some money from us. They didn't report him to the authorities—Pond Bank had no cops anyway—they just confronted him and lectured him.

Numerous families, of different financial and social status, lived in Pond Bank. Two different families owned the two country stores in town and seemed to have some money. Another family, to which my folks Christian witnessed, lived just up the street from us. The husband was an alcoholic, as were many men in the town, but we didn't know that term in those days—he was just a drunk or a person who drank too much. One night the mother and her four small children came running down the little hill to our house, burst in and dove for the nearest closet to hide. The husband and father was cruising up and down the street in his wood paneled Ford station wagon, drunk and shooting his pistol in the air. They were sure that he was going to kill them, and I was sure that he would kill us too. I was twelve or thirteen years old, and this left a deep, scary impression on me. That was my feeling about a lot of the goings-on in Pond Bank.

We lived just on the edge of town, so didn't see a lot of the fights, domestic disputes, arguments, and just bad behavior that occurred in the center of town. Sometimes we didn't know anything about it until a small item appeared in the Chambersburg newspaper, The Public Opinion.

There was a racial tension in the culture. "Negros" were relegated to another small town about three miles from Pond Bank called Brownsville. There were many vile, discriminatory jokes and comments about the people who lived there. Another area at the foot of the mountain was called "String town", which wasn't even a town, but the site of a couple houses occupied by poor folks. A "retarded" black woman, who lived there, was gang raped by a bunch of boys and became pregnant. Behind snickers, the townspeople, with a certain delight, spread rumors of the boys' actions.

The town youth had nothing to do but roam the roads, learn to drink, smoke, steal a few things and have sex at an early age. At school, even the pre-pubescent guys would chase the girls around trying to grope them. A number of the girls got pregnant very young and didn't know who the father was or if they did, the boys took no responsibility. I am sure there were a lot of hidden rapes and abuses among the youth.

Superstitions ran rampant among the villagers. Spooky stories flew through the town like wildfire. The legend of the "White Woman" was a favorite. Periodically, people would see a white figure cross the road in front of their car or see her walking on the railroad tracks at the North end of town. No one knew who she/he was—sometimes pants legs were seen protruding from the bottom of the sheet—intended to do, or why he/she existed, but that didn't deter folks from really believing it was a specter. The legend is of a mother who lost, or threw, her baby, into one of the ponds and she dove in to save it, but before she could retrieve the baby, they both drowned. The White Woman comes back to the town as a ghost looking for her baby. We kids were sure the "White Women" existed; we even saw it streak across the road, lit up by our car's highlights.

In the back yard of our old farmhouse, we had a 100 ft. deep, hand dug well. We had a cistern under the front porch, which was connected to the house plumbing, but we never drank that dirty water. For drinking water at the evening meal, one of us children received the task of bringing a pitcher of water from the well to the table. In the winter, it got dark before supper. The spotlight attached to the house provided a little tunnel of light to the well—a pitch-dark wall encased the beam. We were sure the "White Women" was loitering in the dark and we would run like hell the whole way out and back, careful not to spill too much of the water.

Pond Bank was in the line of the Confederate troops as they, in 1863, stormed their way to Gettysburg, just some fifteen miles east. Stories of their stealing of livestock and food for the troops had been handed down through many generations. I experienced many nightmares of cannons and soldiers fighting on the hills of our farm, probably enhanced by visits to the Gettysburg battlefield. When I couldn't sleep and cried out to Mom, she instructed me to say Bible verses--never to count sheep.

The main purpose of the "mission" church was to "save" the locals. After confessing their sins, accepting Jesus as their Savior and baptized, they joined the church and became Mennonites. Even though they had no heritage of Mennonites, the men were required to wear the "plain " suits to church and the woman to wear the "covering"—"prayer veiling"—all the time. My mother and other women of the church would often have to make some acceptable dresses for these "converts" and men were taken to Mennonite tailors who could alter their suit coat. It seemed quite incongruous to me and the people seemed quite uncomfortable with it.

From the second to the sixth grades of elementary school I attended the Pond Bank—now a two-room schoolhouse—where my grandfather taught for many years. It was his last year of teaching before he retired. Many of the students of Pond Bank were poor and uninterested in education. Numerous ones, mostly boys, would fail class after class and be quite old and grown in the upper grades. My grandpa was a small wry man, about five feet five inches tall, weighing at the most, 135 pounds. But, he had a mean temper, which fired up at misbehavior of the students. He had ample reasons to discipline the students. My mother would tell the story of a large boy who threw a knife at Grandpa who ducked and the knife stuck in the wall behind him.

I will never forget the day that he tried to discipline a student and the student began to sass him back—this was the worst. Grandpa always kept a board in the closet, about three inches wide and about three feet long. He rushed to the closet for his paddle and started to beat the boy on the back while he was sitting in his desk. The boy became more unruly and started to swear at Grandpa who kept beating him until the boy cried for mercy, with painful welts left by the board. However, it was rumored, I don't know it for a fact, that a number of those disrespectful, out of control boys came back to thank him when they became successful members of society, with jobs, family and a average good life. They said that it was my grandfather who finally was an authority that they couldn't disregard and that they were, probably, on the way to landing in jail without his discipline. Such strict discipline today would have landed my grandfather in jail. I never had an issue with Grandpa at school. He showed us no partiality, but then we knew to behave ourselves and escape the wrath. In addition, Daddy said if we got a licking at school, we would get one when we came home.

But there were positive things: Grandpa taught with passion and great knowledge. And we had fun, also. Every morning, we had a period of singing the old folks songs, led by Grandpa and he always read aloud a chapter from an exciting novel. We looked with great anticipation for the next chapter of a mystery novel. This time truly set a wonderful tone for the day. He was an excellent teacher, but just don't cross him.

Homework was a priority for our parents and I never wanted to go to school unprepared. After the chores and dinner, "supper" to us, we children would go into the dining room table and do our homework. Daddy had only an eighth grade education, but Mom finished high school at Eastern Mennonite High School. So, she was always willing to help us with our homework and I think it was a way for her to keep some academics in her life.

For some reason, my second grade was bussed to Duffield School. During that year another health event occurred, a kidney episode of some kind. I don't think it was anything life threatening, but I spent about a week in the hospital, with Mom again saying how special I was that the Lord spared my life.

My first conscience recollection of being aware of my musical desires came around the age of nine. My parents, Daddy in particular, liked telling people that after seeing Eastern Mennonite College (EMC) Professor Mark Stauffer conduct with a baton on an elevated podium, Alfred Gaul's *The Holy City*, I said, that is what I wanted to do when I grew up. The music had a dramatic, emotional effect on me. The entire spectacle of a couple hundred singers and soloist was impressive. There was an aura around Mr. Stauffer, one of grace, elegance and strength that appealed to me.

Soon after that my parents bought an old upright piano. It was a player piano—it played disks with holes in them at appropriate places to create a musical piece when the billows, activated by foot pedals, blew air through them by—but we hardly ever used the player part. It impresses me, now, that they were so insightful of my musical potential that they bought a piano, unusual for a Mennonite family, although not against the rules. I worked on playing "chopsticks"—a familiar piece to beginners--and a few other ditty's by rote and then Paul Nolt, who was a Conscientious Objector serving his two year alternative service—instead of military service—at a nearby tuberculosis sanatorium, who later became my uncle, taught me the basics of reading music at the piano.

The first piece I worked on was a gospel song, "My Jesus, I love Thee" from our Hymnal. First, I learned to pick out the soprano melody with one finger, then added the alto voice part with two fingers on my right hand, and so on, until I could slowly play all four parts with both hands. This was my method of learning to play hymns, until my parents found a teacher for me.

To this day, I am curious why my parents were smart enough to buy me piano lessons, when money was not that plentiful and none of my friends were playing the piano. I don't remember begging them to take lessons, but I remember the enjoyment of making music at the piano. I spent hours and hours doodling at the keyboard.

My parents found a teacher in the nearby town of Fayetteville. She was what I call a "kitchen" teacher, that is, she would be cooking during my lesson and would call in instructions to me, such as: "Honey, that is very good, go on to the next piece" or "Darling, that had too many mistakes in it, play it again". I can't remember if I knew, or my parents knew, that this kind of instruction was not adequate for me.

Somehow they found Miss Dickson, a retired piano teacher from Wilson College, a very respected women's college—maybe they just contacted the college. It was she who introduced me to the great composers and their music. As a farm boy of ten or eleven years, I was so impressed with her old brick house on Lincoln Ave in Chambersburg, her two grand pianos—I assume they were Steinways—her oriental rugs and her perfume. I can still smell that confluence of aromas in her house. She was a bit of a cranky old lady, kind, but insistent of good work.

By that time, I was learning to sight-sing hymns, singing the alto part in my high boy-voice. I sat beside Daddy, on the men's side of the church, and he would help me by pointing out the alto line. Daddy had a very strong tenor voice, although it was not always the most beautiful sound. Not being allowed to have musical instruments in the Mennonite church at that time, meant that we sang a cappella, unaccompanied four-part harmony. There was no piano or organ that played the harmony and all the parishioners sang the melody, as in most churches. Almost everyone in the Mennonite church could sing one part or the other of the four parts, even if it wasn't so accurate or beautiful. The Church valued that kind of singing and decried that bringing in an organ would destroy it.

Singing became a passion for me. I would sing while shoveling shit out of the stables, while on the tractor and while working in the fields—singing the only songs I knew—some of the old familiar gospel songs that we sang in church or heard on recordings. My mother said I sang so loudly over the din of the tractor, while plowing the fields, that I could be heard from the farmhouse, some distance away. Since we weren't allowed to have a radio in the house, we found that if we set the radio on the concrete floor in the garage and rigged it with a piece of wire that served as an antenna, and we could pull in WWVA, Wheeling, West Virginia. Our favorite broadcasts were of the famous male gospel quartets of the time, such as the Blackwood Brothers, the Couriers, and the Statesmen. We would, in addition, spend a lot of time washing Nelson's car since it had a radio built in it.

Amidst the angst of the church life I had a good life. I enjoyed many activities of playing with my family and by myself. Children's mechanized games of today just can't compete with playing a pickup softball game in the pasture by the barn, missing the cow pies as we went after a fly ball or rounding the bases. Horseshoes was a favorite of my Dad and several men from the town. The dining room table, although, too small, served as a Ping-Pong table. Board games were a combination of fun and fights. "Monopoly" was particularly competitive and contentious. In the winter, there was always a jigsaw puzzle in progress. "Rook", a card game with just numbers on the front, replaced regular cards, dubbed "devil cards" because of the suspicion that those weird, evil looking pictures of kings, queens and jacks were evil symbols.

In the winter, skating and sledding were the great sports. Those days they didn't salt the roads, so the "Big Hill", as we called it, was just a quarter of a mile from our house and served as a great sledding site. A fantastic winter event was ice-skating. A number of us went to a farmer's pond, set up a campfire, cleared off the snow, if needed, and enjoyed a great party. Today one would not be allowed to enjoy that, because of liability issues.

The Pennsylvania winters were much harsher than they are now. The light flaky snow piled up quickly and the wind blew it across the open fields until the roads were impassable. Often school was canceled for a couple of days, to our great delight. The drifts were sometimes so deep on our little road that a front loader would have to clear it. Daddy, ever the crude inventor, built a big wooden plow for the back hitch on the Ford tractor and loved "horsing around" pushing the snow out of our driveway around the barn and garage. It was comical because since the plow was on the rear of the tractor, he had to plow backing up.

We made pets of everything. Our cats were barn cats since Mom wouldn't allow animals in the house. Of course, the cats were not neutered, so periodically, we would observe that a cat was growing larger and knew that she was pregnant. One day, she would disappear for a couple days, to come back quite thin, an indication that there was a kitten litter somewhere. The treasure hunt was on. The favorite place for the cats to birth their kittens was a hole in the floor between the mows, created by a broken plank. When the mother cat emerged one day, we would lie on one of those beams above the floor and wait for hours to see if the kittens would come out. In a week or two they ventured out, but were as wild as tigers. As they wandered some distance away from the hole, we quietly moved down the ladder and got between them and the hole. They would hiss, freeze on the spot and we could catch them. Oh, the number of scratches we got from those encounters. But we patiently tamed them, which added to our pets.

We had many dogs—one at a time—often some stray that came around. The farmhouse was separated from all the other farm buildings by a quite busy road. Consequently, our pets frequently got hit by a car and either killed or so injured that they had to be put away—usually shot, because we didn't have the money to take them to a vet. Sometimes, they would miraculously heal on their own. Rusty, a mix of collie and German shepherd, we thought, got hit one day. He crawled into the wagon shed, back into the corner and wouldn't let anyone get near. We put some water and food as close as he would allow, and watched. He dug a slight hole to lie in to recuperate and gradually returned to health all on his own, and emerged with a limp.

We almost always had a couple of Black Angus steers. We really wanted to have a horse, but couldn't afford one, so the next best thing was to ride the steers. Nelson raised rabbits for a while, but more for food and sale than for pets.

The farm life is a great way to grow up, although we often complained about the hard work. But, we gained a sense of responsibility from having to work—the chores had to be accomplished, no excuses. We always had one to three milk cows that required being milked, by hand, morning and evening. When there was more than one cow. a couple of us boys milked, when only one cow, we took turns. The best thing about milking was trying to make as much froth on top of the milk in the pail as possible. To accomplish this, you needed to simultaneously sharply squeeze and pull the udders—teats—to make a highly pressured stream. The barn cats waited for you to try to hit their mouths with a stream of milk. One had to be alert to the cow's tail, often covered with shit, slapping you in the face. Sometimes the cow would lift her foot and tramp it down on your foot or the pail of milk, causing crap to fly in the milk or it would tip over. Milking—always a challenge.

Other chores were feeding the rest of the animals. The hogs needed to be "slopped", the steers fed, the eggs collected and if we had calves, they had to be given a bottle of awful smelling calf formula. Have you ever seen calf shit? It is a foul smelling yellow-green, very runny mess. To this day, when I see that color, I always remark "calf shit yellow".

A couple of years after moving to the farm, we tore down the old one-car garage and built a concrete block building, a rectangular two floor structure that contained three bays on the first floor for cars and an open room on the second floor for chickens. We bought chicks, raised them for the eggs for a couple of generous years and then sent them off for butchering. I hated the chickens and would give them a boot as they crowded around my legs, pecking. Reaching into the nests, particularly when I was too short to see into them often brought surprises of broken eggs, poop, or a cranky old hen pecking your hand to protect her nest. The smell of ammonia from the manure was so rank that it made your eyes water. The windows opened out, but only a small way. To clean out the manure, you had to shove it through several small openings at the bottom of the wall, onto the manure spreader below.

Many of the happiest times of my childhood and youth centered on plying the fields with the little, but mighty, red-bellied, Ford tractor. The best activity was turning over the soil in the spring, with a two-bottom plow, smelling the scent of the fresh earth after the long winter. The crows, black birds and killdeer would jump into the furrows for fresh, live worms. I challenged myself to make the furrows straight, so on the first row, I would focus on a tree a long distance across the field and persistently head for it. Another challenge, actually a danger, came when plowing on the side of the two hills. You would have to—using a flying term—crab up the hill, meaning climbing the hill at an angle so the tractor would not drift down and make the rows crooked.

Shifting gears, up and down the hills and at the ends of the rows presented another self-made challenge. Going up the hills, I attempted to shift to a lower gear as smoothly as possible, without loosing momentum. Arriving at the top of the hills, I shifted back up to a higher gear, just as smoothly. At the end of the row, there grew a "fence row", a mass of uncultivated vegetation—shrubs, small trees and tall grass. The goal was to plow as close to the fencerow as possible and not smash into the growth as you turned. I pulled up the lever that lifted the plow, changed gears and moved the throttle slower in one coordinated motion, turned just shy of the fence, turned into the next furrow and reversed the motion—lower the plow, shift to lower gear, open the throttle. Silly, but a lot of fun.

After the plowing, an implement with big round discs, towed behind the tractor, mashed the lumps of bumpy clods left by the plow. Next, the harrow, with long prongs fastened to a frame was towed over the field to smooth the ground in preparation for the planting of the corn seed.

"Making" hay was a tractor event as well. The hay was mowed down, left to dry, raked into rows for the baler to collect and tie it into bales. Sometimes the baler would shoot the bales directly onto a four wheeled wagon and at other times just dropped them onto the ground. I became involved when I was seven or eight by driving the tractor very slowly among the row of bales as one of my older brothers lifted the bales onto the wagon and the other carefully stacked them. Moving the bales around on a hot, humid summer day was a very dirty, dusty job. The worst came from being stuck in the haymow in the barn, with stifling heat, dust and dirt flying from the bales as you stacked them.

Having such few acres, it wasn't cost effective to own expensive equipment for harvesting our crops. People were hired, with the equipment to bale the hay, pick the corn and harvest the wheat. A machine called a combine cut off the stem of wheat near the ground, striped off the wheat kernels and spit out the chaff—straw—on the ground, which was later was baled and stored in the barn like the hay.

The corn picker machines ran the dried stalk of corn through a trough with augurs that stripped off the ears of corn, husked them and spewed them onto a wagon towed behind. The corn was stored in a corncrib, a long narrow, slated part of the wagon shed, that gave the ears air so they could dry. Dried corn silk wrapped in paper made good "cigarettes" that we secretly smoked in the corncrib.

My parents never had a lot of money, but knew how to stretch the dollar by living on this small farm. The huge gardens yielded most of our vegetables. A lot of our summer was taken up by activities in the gardens, the planting, pulling weeds—we hated it. We enjoyed much more harvesting the crops and aiding in the preparation for canning or freezing. I remember fondly the many times sitting on the front porch at the farm house, as we did in Marion, with the whole family, except Daddy, and sometimes with mother's sisters, husking sweet corn, cutting it off of the cob; shelling peas and beans, peeling peaches from the local orchards. The canned goods were stored in our cellar, one with a dirt floor, on homemade dusty dirty shelves. The potatoes were stored in the "potato bin" that kept them pretty well through the winter, but they needed to be sprouted several times—a dusty dirty job.

Before home freezers, we rented a "locker" in a frozen storage warehouse in Chambersburg for our meats, fruits and vegetables. The trips to the locker were adventures in cold. No matter the temperature outside, you always had to wear overcoats.

All of the parts of a pig or steer were used—pigs' stomachs, pork hocks, beef livers, brains and tongues. "Scrapple" was a mixture of dubious bits of meat compressed together with corn meal—that was fried to a crisp and served with syrup. "pan/pon haus" was traditionally made from all the meat that fell off of the pig head after being boiled for hours. "puddin", a similar mixture of ground meat, also from dubious places, dripped with fat when cooked and was often served with hominy, a corn product. "Dutch goose" was a palatable name for pig stomach. It was stuffed with cubed potatoes and a spicy sausage then roasted, much as one would a goose. We children would fight over the thick end of the stomach, because it was the tastiest. "Souse" was made with various meats, beef tongue, pig hocks, pig head meat, or a combination held together with a rather sour gelatin. Lard was a staple for frying chicken—made the best southern fried chicken in the world—or frying any thing and used in pastries. For many years, lard was considered a very unhealthy food, but some studies now show that it is not as evil as all the artificial stuff we use. I still love this type of food and when we visit relatives in Lancaster County, we go to a meat shop or a butcher and bring home a sampling of those foods in a cooler.

Killing chickens and plucking them was one of those god-awful tasks that you learned was necessary in order to eat them. The head was laid over a wooden chopping block and cut off with a sharp ax. As a kid, it freaked me out to see the chicken jump around without a head until it bled to death—acting like "a chicken with its head cut off". Then the body was dipped into very hot water so the feathers could be plucked. I still get chills as I write this.

We ate very little seafood but, occasionally, Mom fried fish, usually frozen haddock fillet that she cooked to death, which made it so dry that I didn't like fish until later in life. Of course there were the frozen fish sticks, mostly breading with a tough little bit of fish inside. Daddy loved oysters and we had oyster stew and Pond Bank friends taught us how to steam shrimp and that became a special meal. Daddy would tell them, I will buy the shrimp, if you fix them. It became a social event between the two families.

We used anything on the farm that could add to our menu. We had a really old crabapple tree that yielded a lot of wormy fruit. But somehow Mom cut around the holes and pickled them for a treat, as she did watermelon and cantaloupe rind. We dug up the roots of sassafras trees, stripped off the bark and brewed a wonderful tea. Mom brewed root beer, made potato chips, made homemade sauerkraut, baked cakes and cookies. We never felt deprived of any food, but enjoyed the occasional "store bought" item such as olives, candy bars, potato chips, and pretzels.

Hunting provided rabbits, squirrels and pheasants for food. Hunting, a sporting event, for us was a very natural method of getting food as was killing farm animals. Wild life was plentiful on the acres of the farm. We could venture out almost any cool frosty morning in the fall, during hunting season, and kick up a couple rabbits nestled in the small piles of hay left by the baler. Ringed neck pheasants liked scattered corn remaining among the broken corn stalks in the fields and squirrels were plentiful in the nearby woods. Mom fried the rabbits just like southern fried chickens, roasted or fried the pheasants and made squirrel potpie. I didn't realize that all these wild animals were delicacies in some restaurants, particularly the rabbit and pheasant. These were just considered great additions to our food budget.

Daddy strictly taught us about guns. Guns were viewed only as a weapon to hunt animals—not for protection, not for toys, not as a right. The old one-shot 22-caliber rifle was our first gun. When we reached about 12 or so of age, Daddy allowed us to carry the gun but without a bullet in the chamber. It was not sportsman like, but if we discovered a rabbit in a pile of hay, he quietly instructed us to put a bullet in the chamber and we could shoot it. At the age of 15, we boys received our first shotgun, which was a big sign of maturing.

The only toy guns we had as children were a Ping-Pong ball shooting rifle and a couple small plastic water pistols. We never even had a belt with two six-shooter type cap pistols that were authentic looking. We were taught to never play "cops and robbers" or worse yet, "cowboys and Indians". We did sometimes secretly play these games in the woods where our parents couldn't see us, and of course with borrowed toy guns.

Guns were used for pleasure to target shoot. We would set up rows of cans or bottles and try to hit them with the rifle. Skeet shooting was much too expensive so Daddy would bring home a case of rotten eggs. One of us would throw the egg in the air, while another tried to hit it with a shotgun. It was great fun to be the "thrower", to throw it high, to throw it straight forward, to throw it right over the shooter's head. This was particularly fun when, on a holiday like Thanksgiving, Uncle Menno's family would visit and participate.

Daddy was very strict and attentive to safety. We could only carry a gun with the barrel pointing to the ground or up in the air, never over our shoulder holding the barrel or the stock. One of our favorite hunting spots—on abutting property—was some huge piles of tree trunks and branches mixed with a lot of dirt that was pushed there by bulldozers clearing the land. The rabbits had dug burrows throughout the piles. Daddy bought some fox hounds—small dogs that could enter the rabbit holes and flush them out. When the dogs went into the holes in the brush piles, the rabbits would shoot out at odd places at high speeds. It was a challenge to hit them.

One day, I was standing on the pile waiting and my gun fired accidentally, luckily, into the ground. I had forgotten to push on the safety button. Daddy immediately ordered me to the house for the rest of their hunt. I don't think I could emotionally hunt today, but I enjoyed the experience with my Dad. He became more human on those trips with us boys—male time. He might say he had to take a piss, and we snickered behind his back as if he said some really bad swear word or, he would make a joke about finding and extracting the shriveled part of the anatomy needed to pee. Big laughs.

In the summers, as we grew into our teens, we worked at the local cherry, apple and peach orchards. Franklin County, our county, was known for its excellent fruit orchards. Sometimes we picked the fruit, although immigrants, mostly Puerto Ricans were brought in for that. The most fun was driving the flatbed orchard trucks. The top of the cab was sawed off, so that they wouldn't hit the lower branches and injure the fruit. The worst job I had was taking empty peach crates off a conveyor belt and stacking them on pallets. On a hot day, the peach fuzz would fly all over you and itch like crazy, causing me to pray that it would rain and we would have to stop.

Our spiritual lives were a first priority in our family life. At breakfast, Daddy read from his big black Bible, and there was prayer, all of us invited by Daddy at one time or another, to lead the vocal prayer or sometimes he called for silent prayer—each of us offering up our prayer, silently, until he said "amen". Before bedtime, there was "family devotions". We gathered in the living room while Daddy, or sometimes Mother, read from the Scriptures, or a Bible story and we all knelt to pray.

My parents, my mom in particular, lived their lives waiting for the promised return of Jesus to be fulfilled and for the "pie in the sky—Heaven. She frequently talked about heaven, walking the streets of gold, meeting past relatives there, of never experiencing pain again for eternity. The negative news of the day spurred the notion that Jesus was coming soon, and we must be prepared or we will be left behind when the saints rise to heaven. The Bible in Matthew 24:7 says: "You will be hearing of wars and rumors of wars. See that you are not frightened, for those things must take place, but that is not yet the end. For nation will rise against nation, and kingdom against kingdom, and in various places there will be famines and earthquakes". One of my mom's favorite gospel songs said: "This world is not my home, I'm just a passing through. My treasures are laid up some-where beyond the blue. The angels beckon me from Heaven's opened door and I can't feel at home in this world anymore". I feel sorry for Mom—I don't believe she ever was completely happy, or filled with joy without that twinge of guilt that she shouldn't feel it. She felt it was almost sinful to frolic, to hysterically laugh—as Dad did sometimes—or just be silly.

Our parents believed, as the church taught, that the Bible was the inspired Word of God. They believed in the "literal" words of the King James Version, even though it was a translation. Everything in life was measured by what they believed the Bible taught. The Mennonite Church's beliefs stemmed from the Anabaptist movement in the Reformation. Their separation from many of the other religions, such as Presbyterians, Lutherans, and Catholics, was their belief in adult baptism, not infant baptism. They believed that a person needed to reach the age of "accountability"—understanding intellectually and emotionally, the spiritual concepts of the sin, guilt, forgiveness, etc.—before "accepting Jesus as their personal Savior", be "born again", be baptized and accepted into the church.

In the 50s and 60s, that seemed to be negated as the age of "accepted" accountability sagged lower and lower. I accepted Jesus, as my personal Savior and was baptized, when I was only nine years old. Although I was a pretty smart kid, I'm sure that I didn't fully comprehend the meaning of sin, accountability, responsibility salvation, etc.

As I look back, I really can't separate much of my parents' personalities, moral values, ethics, child discipline and life style, from their Mennonite faith. We were Mennonite, not Amish. We had all the modern conveniences, but we dressed "plain"—the men, after being "converted", were required to wear a "plain" suit coat, the lapel cut off and the collar tailored to look much like a Nehru jacket.

The women members were required to wear the "prayer veiling"—also, called "the covering"—a net like material that covered most of their hair which was gathered up in some kind of "bun" at the back of the head. They also, had to wear a "cape" on their dresses, an additional vest-like outfit that was meant to be more modest, to deemphasize the breast—to minimize men's lust.

This "different" method of dressing was to visually distinguish us from the "world". Mennonites, at that time, believed in the tenet of "non-conformity" with the world. It came from the Scriptures such as: "Be ye not conformed to this world, but be ye transformed by the grace of God" (Romans 12:2) and "If ye were of the world, the world would love his own: but because ye are not of the world, but I have chosen you out of the world, therefore the world hateth you." (John 15:19)

My parents took to heart the reported Scripture: "Spare the rod and spoil the child", which I heard many times that it is in the Bible, but actually is a quote from Samuel Butler, a 17th century poet. Mom never spanked us, but uttered the threat: "Wait until your father comes home". Usually this was in response to Nelson and me, fiercely fighting, for disobedience and refusing to do a chore. I look back now and understand that when Daddy came home from a long day; the last thing he wanted to hear was of our bad behavior. No wonder, the lickins' were quite severe, at times. In good weather, we often had to cut the switch off of a tree.

One time, probably around twelve or thirteen, I took off running down through the garden, with Daddy in hot pursuit. I got about half way through the garden, and I remember thinking, if I am going to do this, I would have to keep running forever. I stopped and the punishment had some extra sting in it, I am sure. We were only allowed to cry for a certain length of time, no over indulging pity allowed. His favorite phrase, when we cried other than for a lickin' was, "If you don't stop crying, I'll give you something to cry about".

We sang together, for years, as a family—Mom sang soprano, my two older brothers sang bass and Daddy sang a strong tenor and I sang alto, my sister sang alto when she was old enough to join. I remember that I was so young that I had to stand on something, so I could see the music that they held. We sang at numerous area church services and gatherings. We never thought of getting paid. We sang the old gospel songs, like the gospel quartets of the day, found in books that my parents had collected. These songs were more complicated and interesting than the congregational hymns. Many had lead-in lines for one voice or other, with responses by the other voices, in a way that gave some solo lines to each voice. While singing an inner voice, alto—a cappella—I developed my ear and sense of pitch.

I played "church" with my brother, Nelson,---he was the preacher and I was the song leader. From a young age, I liked to conduct pieces on LP recordings of Mormon Tabernacle Choir, the Billy Graham Crusade Choir or the Mennonite Hour Chorus, a radio choir that I conducted as a senior in college. I don't remember how I conducted in those early years, but must have just copied the song leaders.

When I was in sixth grade, the county education board announced that next year we would be bussed to Chambersburg to a new consolidated junior high school. A new high school had been built for a consolidated student body and the old high school would now house the junior high, grades seven through nine. It was announced that in order to field a band that first fall, instrumental lessons would be offered free of charge. I desperately wanted to take up the trumpet. There was something majestic and strong about the trumpet that drew me to it. My parents decided that the uniformed band with its marches was too similar to a military exercise for us Mennonites to become involved. It would mean some practice after school hours that would interfere with chores. This was not the era of "schlepping" children around to many sports, musical events, and concerts. Likewise, I was prohibited from joining the choirs because the girls wore low cut gowns and the boys white tuxes. The music director persisted in trying to recruit me, because he knew from music class that I could sight sing very well and had a good voice.

Moving to a big city school was a huge scary step for me, way out of our family comfort zone—many unknowns. There was the bus ride, the changing of classes, a huge student population, many different teachers, and mostly non-Mennonite students. So far, in my life, most things were predictable following my parents' experiences.

Consolidated public school was an enigma for me. I envied those students who could participate in all the school activities, music ensembles, dances, and dating. I was embarrassed that I wore plain suits and never wanted my few non-Mennonite friends to see me in it. Most of my friends were Mennonites, who waited together for the school buses. I had a couple friends, from homeroom or classes. Sam, who drove a cool pickup truck would collect me, some days, as I exited the school bus and we drove around until school actually began. Real cool!

I watched the students dance in the gym at lunchtime, as I ate my packed lunch on the bleachers. I envied the seemingly, comfortable closeness between boy and girl as they touched during the dance. I lusted after the cute girls in flowing short skirts and bobby socks.

Daddy continued to drive the store truck after we moved to Pond Bank. He worked long days, getting up around five o'clock, and driving the some twelve miles to the warehouse early enough to finish loading the truck and heading out. He arrived home, usually, around 6:00 p.m. ate supper and, in the summer, worked in the garden until dark.

It was a treat accompanying Daddy and helping, even though it meant getting up so early. Leaving that early, we didn't bother with breakfast, but waited until arriving at the warehouse for the "healthy" breakfast of doughnuts and awful, percolated, strong coffee, even at the age of ten or twelve. I helped load the truck to overflowing, for the day. There were always adventures on the trip, such as chasing down a groundhog with a pop bottle—groundhogs were a most hated beast by farmers—stopping to talk to a farmer making hay, some special food treat, etc.

The women customers came from the house, climbed the steps at the back of the truck, stood in the aisle and read off their grocery list. He knew exactly where to find it. I knelt on the driver's seat with a bill pad, Daddy called out the items and the prices, which we wrote on the pad, and when the lady was finished, I challenged myself to see how fast I could total up the list. Most of the time, however, Daddy did it because he was very good at addition, with so much practice over the years. I bet that he could have won a race with early calculators.

I had the responsibility of helping to fill the bags with the groceries in the proper manner—with Daddy, there was always a proper way to do anything—and carry them into the house for the women.

Daddy was a bit of a tease and a flirt and the women loved him, so sometimes he would linger for a conversation. If I was lucky, the TV would be broadcasting in the house and I would take the opportunity to watch. Saturdays were the best because a cartoon or a show like "Gunsmoke" was on.

Noon meal, "dinner", was always interesting. Daddy sliced some lunchmeat, or broke open a can of sardines, or Vienna sausages for sandwiches. There were always bananas, "pop"—soda—or Daddy made some great, fresh lemonade from real lemons, and on very hot days a Popsicle. Then it was naptime. Between the driver's seat and the front left side of the truck, there was a space just big enough for a little bed, often a crate that had been filled with bananas, just the packing straw remaining as bedding. Daddy sat on the driver's seat with his head back, fall asleep in two minutes, sleep fifteen minutes, wake up without an alarm, always seeming refreshed to go on with the day. He drove that store truck for 24 years until the super market grocery stores came on to the scene and, even rural folks were more mobile.

My parents were intent upon teaching us the value of hard work and money. I don't remember the age, but they always paid us a generous allowance. Although it wasn't directly tied to our work, we knew we had to work. Daddy's phrase, "If you don't work, you don't eat" supposedly came from someplace in the Bible. I remember that in my teens I was paid five dollars, which in the 50's was a lot of money. With that, I was expected to buy all that I needed—if any left over what I wanted. A number of times, however, I remember not having enough money to buy the amount of new school clothes that Mom thought I should have and she took me to Penny's and she bought some.

I learned another important lesson when I thought I had to buy a taillight for my bike. It looked like a traffic light, operated by battery that shone green while peddling, yellow while coasting and red when breaking. I never did get it working properly and it now is still in some covered trash heap someplace, as it was made of metal and plastic.

In my teen years, the Christian life became a struggle between good and evil, between Heaven and Hell, between normal human tendencies and Christian taboos. I struggled with the Christian/Mennonite concepts, the restriction of the church and its interpretation of the Bible, sex, self-image and guilt.

Sex, as for many pre-and pubescent youth was an issue, but was compounded by the ranting and raving, from ministers, about the evils of sex and even the "lusting in your hearts".

In the winter while ice-skating, even though we were bundled up with layers of clothing, it didn't prevent me from enjoying the closeness of our bodies as I skated with a girl. We would cross arms as we skated in rhythm around in circles and cuddle by the ever-present roaring fire.

For a number of summers I went to Laurelville Mennonite Camp, located in the small mountains near Pittsburg, Pennsylvania. first for boys' week and then mixed gender week. It was a chance to interact with other Christian youth, to participate in sports, music, and social games. The facilities were quite rugged, log cabins for sleeping, a large wooden structure containing the dining hall—I can still smell many of those aromas. During the mixed gender weeks, a lot of the cool guys and gals "dated". I was envious, but too shy to really participate. It was one of the first times I felt the isolation from main stream Mennonites, living in Pond Bank. The kids from other areas seemed so cool, socially confident and mature.

During those weeks, a great deal of emphasis was laid on the Christian life dos and don'ts—mostly don'ts--with services every night calling out the sins of the world and life. There were classes during the day, espousing the Christian faith as they, the Mennonite counselors, saw it. There were sessions on sex. And doubt me not, they in the 50's, still used scare tactics of masturbation causing brain damage, and health risk due to loss of blood through the semen. Of course, they taught that physical contact of any kind could/would lead to intercourse.

An interesting and humorous side story. My parents never had the "birds and bees" talk. I think they knew that camp was handling that part of our Christian education. But they did buy us a book called, Christian Manhood, written by two Mennonite Doctors. I still have it just for grins. Here are some of the chapter headings and subheadings:

PROBLEMS FACING GROWING MANHOOD
Influence of Evil Companions—Masturbation or Self-abuse
Other Wrong Sex habits and Teachings
CHRISTIAN STANDARDS IN COURTSHIP
Love and Physical Passion
THE PITFALLS AND DANGERS OF COURTSHIP
Worldly Standards vs. Christian Standards
Worldly Pleasures vs. Christian Courtship

It's amazing I'm wasn't' and am not more screwed up than I am.

However, one of my brothers was digging through my mother's lingerie drawer—I don't know why—and discovered a brown covered book called, Sane Sex Life. This became a book much sought after when my parents were away. We would carefully place it back exactly where we found it, so they didn't know we knew. This was quite an advanced sex book for that time—the 50s and for a Mennonite couple. It was sort of like that period's The Joy of Sex. There were few or no pictures, but quite descriptive guidebook for "Sane Sex". It described foreplay, positions and how to give your partner pleasure and more.

Our parents would have been horrified if they knew we had read it. But, the night before each of our weddings, Mom came with a brown bag that held "The Book". By the time of my wedding and my sister's wedding, it was a big joke and our older brothers would say: "Did you get The Book?" As one of my brothers said, "Did they think we would read it like a recipe book that night before having sex"? Many sibling chuckles!

In most Mennonite churches, revival meetings were a highlight of the church year. Evangelistic/revival meetings were at the heart of keeping up with one's spiritual life--to be reminded of our sinful nature and take stock. They occurred twice a year with a guest evangelist, usually an itinerant evangelist from out of the area. The more fiery, dramatic, and emotional the minister orated, the greater his respect and popularity.

Grandpa Shank was one of those fiery, very popular preachers on that revival circuit. When he gave up teaching, he traveled a great deal. He could rock your socks with very descriptive language.

One of my parents' favorite evangelists was a small man, wiry and very dramatic. He shouted to dramatically emphasize the meaning of sin, death, the after life, heaven and hell. He jumped up and down, left the pulpit and walked down the aisle flailing his arms.

I remember he and other evangelists screaming—"Do you remember the pain from burning just the tip of your finger on the stove—this is how it will be over your WHOLE body through ETERNITY in Hell". You can imagine how that scared the hell out of a nine year old boy and I rushed to the front of the church to receive my Lord Jesus and ask His forgiveness for all the sins that I had committed—mostly looking at girl's breasts beneath the "cape" and lusting. Some of my other sins were: telling some little white lies, saying very mild expletives, smoking corn silk cigarettes, disobeying my parents, and fighting with Nelson. I never felt good enough, "filled with the Spirit," or "free from the bondage of sin".

The "invitation" was a very sacred ritual. At the very end of a revival service, after the hell-fire sermon, the preacher gave the "invitation", a call for all those in the congregation who were unsaved, or had "backslid"—backslid meaning reneged on some of the baptismal vows—to publicly confess and repent by standing up, or raising your hand, or going to the front of the church and kneel at the altar.

There was always the morbid hymn sung to prick one's conscience, to remind you of all the evil deeds you had done. Many times the "invitation" went on and on with the singing of all the verses of several poignant hymns and then extended further by humming the last hymn a time or two. One of the favorites was "Just as I am, without one plea, and that One's blood was shed for me. And as He bids me come to Thee, O Lamb of God, I come, I come". Right now as I write that, I can recall that dreadful feeling of guilt and remorse.

Often the evangelist would say things like, "The Holy Spirit is telling me there is someone in the audience who needs to get right with the Lord. He might not get a second chance—he may have an accident on the way home—where would he spend eternity?" That always got me, because I just knew he was talking about me. I raised my hand, many times to the "invitation", because of the guilt that was implanted in my young mind. I never felt righteous enough; I would kneel by my bed for a lengthy period of prayer--as the "righteous" people related in testimonies—but I would fall asleep. We were told if we were "sanctified"—never understood what that meant—we wouldn't be tempted. There were testimonies of walking with Jesus everyday—never had that experience, either

The "unpardonable sin" was the strongest threat from the pulpit. If you resisted the "Holy Spirit" too often, He would stop calling you and you would then feel no more guilt. This condemned you to a life of sin and damnation.

Summers brought numerous tent revival meetings to the area. We traveled as far as 80 – 100 miles, to hear my parents' favorite evangelists: George R. Brunk, Howard Hammond and Myron Augsburger. Brunk, Hammond and Augsburgers' teams would erect huge tents in a Mennonite farmer's field for their "Revival Meetings". This week of nightly services were huge events for the Mennonites, but other Christians attended also. A whole circus atmosphere encompassed these events, with big semis hauling the tents and all the equipment—chairs, stage, sound systems, and toilets. Many Mennonite men worked for a day to set up the tents—no elephants there. Sawdust was spread in the aisles of the tent, giving off a wonderful aroma of wood. When one responded to the invitation by going to the front of the tent, it was called, "going down the sawdust trail".

Amidst the shameful exploitative guilt, the Mennonite faith has some deeply held beliefs that I embrace in my spiritual life to this day. Mennonite faith values the horizontal relationship with our fellow human beings, as important as that vertical relationship with God. The Bible relates the story of the Pharisees—the church leaders—who tried to give Jesus, what they thought, would be a trick question—"What is the greatest Commandment"? Jesus answered, "Thou shalt love the Lord thy God with all thy heart, and with all thy soul, and with all thy mind, and the second is like unto it, Thou shalt love thy neighbor as thyself". (Matthew 22:37-38) That puts the horizontal and the vertical relationships on an even plane.

The importance of that horizontal relationship taught me about the sin of discrimination, and of prejudice. As stern as Grandpa Shank was with discipline and religion, he had a soft spot for the "Negros". He often preached of the horrible sin of slavery, becoming so emotional at times that he had to pause so he wouldn't break down. He was very proud that his son, my Uncle Luke, who attended and received a Masters degree from Tuskegee Institute and was one of the few whites on campus. Booker T. Washington was one of the influential blacks to create Tuskegee. My parents took me to a number of black choir concerts, including one by the Tuskegee Glee Club. This all made a deep impression on me for the rest of my life.

Another event that led to questions about black and white people issues was a journey to Tampa, Florida in 1956. Wilmer was serving his two-year alternative service instead of military service, by teaching in a Mennonite school in Tampa. He was engaged, so at Christmas we all piled in our 1953

Oldsmobile and took Mary Louise, his fiancé, with us to visit him.   This was my first big trip in general and particularly to the South.   I remember when we stopped in Alabama or Georgia for gas, I couldn't understand the native that serviced our car, his accent was so thick; one I had never heard before. The segregation of everything left me mystified and disturbed. I had heard about it, but still was blown away with the "colored" water fountains and the "white" water fountains, the separate rest rooms, businesses with "no coloreds" permitted signs, including restaurants. I just couldn't' reconcile that with our belief that God created everyone and our constitution states that "all men were created equal".

We were very skeptical of other denominations—particularly Catholics. Our concept was that Catholics weren't allowed to read the Bible for themselves, who had a weird ritual that was called "The Mass", performed in Latin. We thought it strange that they had to go to the priest for confession and couldn't talk to God directly, that they worshipped the Virgin Mary as much as Jesus and practiced infant baptism, on and on.

There were a number of Pentecostal Churches—Assembly of God—commonly called "Holy Rollers" in the area. They held tent evangelistic meetings in Pond Bank or nearby towns in the summer, broadcasting over huge loudspeakers, so loud that we could sit out on our porch and hear them clearly. Quite a few people we knew attended one of the Pentecostal churches and as a gesture of friendship and respect, we attended a service. Wow! The goings-on in that service scared the life out of me. I had never seen people speak in tongues and lose themselves in the "Spirit". To me as a ten – twelve year old, it was very troubling.   I saw a schoolmate of mine have an epileptic seizure and this seemed very similar and I was deeply frightened. The people leapt up, yelled and screamed gibberish, frothed at the mouth, rolled in the aisles, lifted their hands, while someone would interpret. It didn't seem like a Holy experience to me and I was very negatively impressed, adding to the confusion about the spiritual life.

Twice a year, at Pond Bank Church, we observed the ritual of Communion, which included the "washing of feet", a humble symbol of our relationship with others. At the Sunday morning service the week prior, everyone who was "saved" and wanted to participate in Communion had to publicly confirm their faith or confess their sins. Everyone eligible—meaning those who were baptized in the Mennonite faith—was required to stand and say "I am right with my God and my fellowmen and I expect to take communion". Taking communion, when you were living with known unconfessed sins would "bring damnation to your soul". I remember numerous times, a person confessed, on the spot, some bad feelings between he/she and another person or some admission of committing a sin.

Communion involved my parents, since my father was the Deacon, in preparation for the service. Red grape juice, instead of wine, represented the blood of Jesus and crust-less bread represented the body of Jesus. We drank from a common cup—not individual cups—for the juice, passing it from person to person through the pews and then filing to the front of the church to receive the bread.

Next came the feet washing ritual. Prepared basins of warm water were brought out to the front benches. To us young people, it was a bit creepy. We usually chose another young person to partner with, but if you were an odd person out, you might end up with someone weird. One person knelt down over the basin and put the sitting person's feet in the water, splashed water over them, toweled them dry and they switched positions to repeat the ritual. Then came the "Holy Kiss", instructed some place in the Bible. Most often it was a kiss on the cheek, but there was at least, one creepy man who tried to kiss you on the lips, and we avoided him like the plague.

My musical training continued to develop in my teenage years. My piano instruction became a constant joy and growth. I enjoyed practicing—probably never enough to totally thrive. My brother, Nelson, did not enjoy practicing and Mother had to prod him, many times, to sit at the piano and play. I hated when he practiced, because he made so many mistakes and kept repeating them over and over again.

Since singing in the church was a cappella, a song leader stood in front of the congregation and "led" the hymns. The man—of course no women were allowed—walked to the front of the church, gave the hymn number, waited for the parishioners to find it, blew the tonic note on a pitch pipe, sang the beginning note for all the four parts, then led by singing the melody with the sopranos, while conducting. I'm not sure why a cappella singing was so important to our type of Mennonites—the Bible speaks of praising God with lyre, harp and cymbals—except that it was traditional and really quite wonderful. There were more liberal thinking Mennonite Churches that began to have organs. We thought that the organ would destroy our special singing. The irony is that it wasn't the organ that destroyed our a cappella singing, but the bands with loudly amplified guitar, keyboard and drums that have come into the church to perform the god awful Christian rock and folksongs sung in unisons.

The church held summer "singing schools" that taught the fundamentals of music theory—key and time signatures, lines and spaces, beat patterns for conducting the most common meters: 3/4, 2/4, 4/4, 6/8.

For years, hymns were only written in shaped notes—a different shape for every pitch of the diatonic scale. People became quite proficient in sight singing by this method. In about 1953 the national church music committee published a new hymnal with all round notes. My parents, as well as many others became very frustrated as this took away their ability to read music quickly. The singing school had already transitioned to round notes by the time I studied—I never did learn to read shaped notes. It's interesting that there are now some shaped note societies that gather to spontaneously sing songs in shaped notes.

I was about 14 years old when I began to lead singing in church. I loved it—it came very naturally to me—I thrived on it, making me more certain of my still limited musical aspirations.

Lancaster Mennonite School 1958 - 1960

My whole life changed when I transferred to Lancaster Mennonite School (LMS). My brother, Wilmer, graduated from LMS and I don't know what exactly entered into that decision but, it set the precedent for all of us to attend a Mennonite high school for our last two years only, since it was quite expensive. I know that my parents were worried about the "worldliness" of the public schools and Mom had graduated from Eastern Mennonite High School. Mom was always interested in education and how it might propel us into a good profession.

The dorm at LMS became my home during the week and I rode home on Fridays with a carload of students from the Chambersburg area, for the weekends. At last, I was able to participate in everything: sports, music, and a social life. Interaction with girls was severely limited by the administration with very strict rules of behavior. We were not allowed to, openly, have girl-friends. Caught talking alone with the same girl too frequently resulted in a letter from the dean of boys, being sent home to parents. My parents received, at least, one of those letters, but, thank god, never took it too seriously. There were ways of sneaking around the Dean and have conversations with the same girl, by playing ping pong together, by simply walking together to classes, eating meals together at the same table or ice skating in the winter. The Mill Stream meandered through the campus and froze solid enough in the winter so that we could skate for about a half of mile.

I could date on weekends, driving some distances to meet the girl that I liked from LMS. My parents trusted me enough to give me one of their cars to have dates with my girlfriend. Since we couldn't go to movies and other venues off-limits, dates were often associated with church and music, attending church services, a sacred concert or "Singings—gatherings of people who just wanted to sing—hymns and gospel songs, often led by some well-known local song leader. Of course, relations with girls were quite platonic occasions. The church believed that pre-marital sex was a serious transgression. As mentioned, any physical contact might lead to that activity, so holding hands was stretching the principle and kissing was forbidden. I had decided that I would not kiss until engaged. But in college, in a very serious relationship—although not engaged—I did have my first kiss.

One very significant musical event occurred when I attended my first concert of a classical performance—a performance of Handel's *Messiah*, performed in a concert hall in Harrisburg, Pennsylvania. My date and I went with several other dating couples from my class at LMS. It was the first time that I had seen a choral group and soloists accompanied by an orchestra. Wow! What an impression it engendered! This music tapped deeply into my soul, the first awaking to the great music of the world, not just gospel music or hymns, adding another step on the ladder of my growing reality of music, increasing minutely to my knowledge of the wealth of those musical works.

On the LMS campus, a strict dress code ruled. The girls' skirts and dresses were required to be of a certain length, their dresses were measured from the floor to the bottom hem, to be certain that they weren't too short. They were required to wear a certain type—shape and size—of "prayer veiling" on their heads, covering most of their hair. Boys could wear most anything to school, but were required to close the top button on their shirts. For dress up, a regular suit was allowed, but only a bow tie, not a long tie. Individual churches, as mine, still required the plain suit. Questions arose in my mind as I saw, for first time, that other devout, believing Mennonite youth, when away from campus, dressed differently from me, some even wearing long ties with the normal suit. When not on campus, many girls wore smaller prayer veiling with hair protruding around the edges. Could they be going to Heaven, also? Did being separate from the world have a different meaning than I was led to believe from my sheltered Pond Bank life?

Starting my junior year, instead of my freshman year, created some difficulty in breaking into the social fabric of the school. Students had already settled into the roles of song leader, members of quartets, sextets, student administration, etc. It took a while for me to have the opportunity to show my talent as a musician, but I auditioned and was accepted into men's and mixed choruses. I started leading singing in our small, evening prayer meetings. From all the practice of song leading at Pond Bank church, I demonstrated my skill as a passionate and competent leader. This led to the big stage, leading singing at the required daily chapel services for the whole student body. I completely threw myself into the musical life of the school and continued to develop as a musician. Most students came from the Mennonite tradition of a cappella singing which contributed to very fine choirs.

My voice changed to a man's lower and deeper sound late and slowly, so I sang tenor. My choir director, although well intentioned, did me a disservice by advising that I should continue to sing tenor during the process and I would become a permanent tenor. Everyone wants to be a tenor—more sought after than basses—thus I continued squeezing out the high notes with increasing difficulty. For example, the high "A" for tenors in "The Heaven's are Telling" from Haydn's *Creation* still hurts in my throat even when I conduct it.

I dated a few times, a girl with a fine soprano voice and as usual we went to a church service. During a hymn, I sang bass instead of tenor, because it was more comfortable, after which she commented, "You have a lovely bass voice, why don't you sing bass in choir"? When I entered college as a music major, my voice teachers confirmed that I certainly was not a tenor.

Even though I was in all the select choruses at LMS, frequently led singing and had a good voice, I had an inferiority complex to those with more experience. I was very envious of the popular senior quartet and octet. I realized, again, what a different background I had, growing up in Pond Bank, in a small mission church rather than from the big, traditional Mennonite churches of Lancaster County. But, perhaps it made me more determined to be successful. From my senior class at LMS, about five people went on to receive advanced degrees in music, but I am the only one with the doctorate and many professional experiences.

A big health event occurred one of the weekends in the fall of my senior year, I was cleaning shit out of a stable when I became very faint. I went to the house and Mom thought it was possibly a flu that was going around and I should go to bed. The next morning, I had to lean over the bed, to keep from fainting, while putting on my pants. When I headed down the stairs, I did faint and my family, at the breakfast table, rushed to me as they heard a loud thump at the landing at the bottom of the steps.

Mom sent me to lie on the sofa in the living room and called the doctor as soon as he had office hours. On the doctor's examining table, I again fainted and he had to catch me to keep me from falling on the floor. I was rushed to the Chambersburg hospital, by ambulance, where they discovered that I had bled profusely internally. They had to give me a blood transfusion of eight pints of blood over a number of days.

They diagnosed it as a bleeding stomach ulcer and put me on a very bland diet and lots of milk. At LMS, I had to go to the house of the boy's dorm manager every couple hours to drink a glass of milk. Special mashed food that looked like baby food was made especially for me in the dining hall. Very embarrassing. In those days, they thought that my ulcer was caused by stress; taking too many Aspirin for the cold, or something that I ate that scratched the stomach lining. This was very different from today, where scientific evidence shows that bacteria caused it.

Mom had a reason, again, to think that I was special and was allowed to live for a spiritual reason. I know my siblings got tired of hearing that poor Carroll was so very special.

After graduating from high school and having been accepted into Eastern Mennonite College, I needed a job to earn money to help pay for college. My parents promised to pay one quarter of my costs each year—the first quarter. The cost of a year of college at that time, I guess, was around $6,000.

After the leaving the store truck, Daddy became a salesman, of petroleum products and paints for Central Petroleum Company (CEN-PE-Co). So,

Daddy knew a lot of farmers, tractor dealers, and construction workers—all who used equipment that needed oil, oil and gas treatments. He, also, sold paints and roof coatings, for barns and sheds.

One of his customers was an Oliver tractor dealer, with quite a large business. That first summer after Lancaster Mennonite School, Daddy and I went into his shop one day and Daddy asked:

"Do you have something this young man can do for the summer?"
Owner: "Well, can he drive a truck"?
Daddy: "Sure, he can drive anything".
Owner: "OK, I might just have the job. Show up on Monday, young man".

The farm did give me experience driving farm equipment and some smaller trucks, but nothing like an 18-foot flatbed truck loaded with a heavy tractor. I showed up on Monday, for the first day of work, a little intimidated and scared, but pretty sure of myself. My first assignment was to deliver a large Oliver tractor to a farmer some 25 miles out into the country.

The truck was a contrary old beater, 18-foot flat bed International, vintage about 1950. It was well used. For whatever strange reason—remember the tractor shifting—I had developed an obsession for shifting gears, quickly and smoothly. Well, 1950 was long before synchronized gears. The old truck was "cantankerous as an animal in heat"—we would say on the farm.

So, with the big Oliver on the truck, I proceeded down the rural roads. Going through the little farm towns was embarrassing—at every stop sign, I would grind the hell out of the gears—I was sure the old farmers and town folks loitering on the street corners were laughing at me. I was determined to conquer this old beast of a truck through the summer, but he just wouldn't let me. I was successful, at times, with a smooth shifting of the gears, but never consistently.

The guys at the shop were a rough bunch, and, of course, knew I was Mennonite and assumed, correctly, that I was a virgin. They, further, learned that I was going off to college in Virginia. They loved to tease and laugh at me: "Wait till those southern corn crackers (loose girls) git (sic) ahold of you. They'll take care of you."

The next summer, I worked at a lumberyard—another of Daddy's customers—driving newer flatbeds and dump trucks. We had to load and unload most of them by hand, although they did have a forklift in the lumberyard for some things. The worst part entailed trying to look busy when there wasn't much business. The best part, other than driving the trucks, was noontime, sparking a lively game of horseshoes.

The rest of the summers, I worked for a builder, a family friend from Pond Bank. He was a building perfectionist, from whom I learned a lot of skills and he was very patient in teaching me, but I can't tell you how often I had to redo or repaint something because it was not done well enough. With this experience, I remodeled most of the houses that I owned over the years, and saved a lot of money.

Many of my college pals spent summers in adventures, such as, following the wheat harvest from the southern plains North, or working in the salmon canneries of Alaska—hard work, but good money. I so wanted to experience that, but it was too risky for my parents.

College years 1960 - 1964

As graduation from Lancaster Mennonite High School approached, I began to think about college, as did most of my friends. I didn't have the typical options of looking at a number of schools, evaluating their music programs, applying to several and choosing one. I didn't even know that was the normal method among high school grads. There really was only one choice, Eastern Mennonite College (EMC), acceptable to my parents and besides, I would have been scared to death to venture into a secular college or university. Even other Mennonite colleges, like Goshen College in Indiana, were much too liberal for my family—liberal meaning too lax dress codes, dating practices, social activities, and musical instruments. I don't remember auditioning at EMC. There probably wasn't one, so I was accepted on my grades.

I began as a music major, but wasn't sure I had enough talent to succeed. I was quite weak in theory and I was not confident of my vocal potential. Freshman theory proved difficult for me, even though I had a basic knowledge from Singing School and piano lessons. The ear training part—dictation of melodies, chords and pitch intervals—came slowly to me.

I made a commitment to myself to earn at least a "B" in theory or I would drop music as a major. I didn't know what major I would choose, but thought about a Bible major—can't imagine that now. I managed to earn a "B", but EMC only had a total of ten hours of music theory classes and I sensed—why, I don't know—that this wasn't adequate and even though I hated theory, I enrolled in two more semesters at nearby James Madison University in Harrisonburg, which had an excellent music program.

Feeling insecure from only attending Mennonite institutions, I was intimidated to test myself against "real" music majors and an excellent, but tough, professor on a secular campus. So I wouldn't be late to the first class, I drove to and around the campus a week before to survey the campus and find my classroom. With fear and trembling, I entered that first class. I worked my butt off and, again, managed to make a "B". That experience greatly increased my self-concept and confidence—I was pretty proud that I succeeded in a music course at a real, secular university.

My first voice lessons at EMC were in a Class Voice of about eight students, with J. Mark Stauffer, an icon in the Mennonite musical arena, but not a great soloist or music teacher. In fact, a few years later, he became a minister and pastored as chaplain, at hospitals and retirement homes. When my parents moved to Mennonite Haven, a retirement home in Chambersburg, after my Dad's illness, he was their chaplain. I gained a great respect for him as a spiritual leader and counselor.

I had my first private voice lessons with Earl Maust. Maust was just finishing up his doctorate, thus much more current in vocal literature and pedagogy than Stauffer. Needing a piano for my songs' accompaniments required a trip to Maust's house, just at the edge of this small campus, in order to use his spinet, upright piano, since instruments were banned from the campus. I had no background in vocal training or vocal literature, but luckily Mr. Maust instructed by first building good vocal technique and began my study with the old Italian arias from the G. Schirmer yellow book, that many teachers, including myself, use today.

My enjoyment of vocal study grew as I began to sing the great literature of the Romantic Art Song repertoire. There was little mention of opera in EMC's program and I don't remember singing one operatic aria during my years there—I did sing a couple of arias from Handel's Messiah.

Since there were no pianos on campus and no faculty member capable of giving piano lessons, I went off campus and studied private piano, with a cousin-in-law that had minimal classical piano training. By my junior year, I decided I was not progressing enough, and again went to James Madison to study piano with a fine pianist and teacher, Miss Integer. By then, a small piano was moved into a practice room at EMC and I could practice there. I certainly wasn't becoming a great pianist, but I was learning a great deal about composers, piano literature, and theory.

Another step up the rung of the ladder to greater musical knowledge came from attending the community concert series in Harrisonburg. It was quite traditional of EMC students, particularly music students, to buy a season's ticket. Having limited acceptable events for dating, this was a great opportunity to attend something off-campus on dates. Attending these concerts exposed me to some of the best performers of that era—Rise Stevens, Richard Crooks, the Russian Cossacks, Rubinstein, Roger Wagner Chorale, to mention a few. These events gave me a clue to the great world of beautiful, spine chilling music and instilled in me the desire to be a part of it, even though I didn't have an inkling of how I would accomplish that.

I also joined the Columbia Record Club—LPs, of course. My first record was a performance of Purcell's *Trumpet Concerto*, and the Vivaldi *Double Trumpet Concerto*. Recordings of Classical Pops with the Boston Pops and Arthur Fiddler introduced me to many of the popular, standard classical pieces. Recordings followed with works I, by that time, needed to be familiar with such as, Vivaldi's *Four Seasons*, Mozart's *Eine kleine Nachtmusik*, Grofe's *Grand Canyon Suite*, and Tchaikovsky's *1812 Overture*, Handel's *Water Music* and *Royal Fireworks Suite*.

Since EMC was a religious Mennonite school and the choral groups' concert tours performed only in churches, our programs contained only sacred, a cappella music. We did sing some secular music in various informal programs on campus.

Through out much of my career I had the "Imposter Syndrome" described in a book by John Graden. Even though my talent was confirmed in many ways, I always felt that I was not as good as people thought I was and, some time I would be discovered as an "Imposter".

One of the most affirming events was my selection as student conductor, each college year, of every chorus of which I was a member. My task was to rehearse the choir when the conductor was absent, without a piano. Even though I was weak in theory, I was able to hear pitch problems and wrong notes without the help of an accompaniment. I would be wary of trying that today.

Having no instruments on campus disallowed any instrumental ensembles—no orchestra, no string quartets, and none of the great, choral masterworks with orchestra. We did perform *The Holy City*, by Alfred R. Gaul—sung a cappella, even though, scored for orchestra accompaniment. This performance became an annual occurrence, mixing current students and alumni who were invited to return and sing. The solos sounded very austere without an accompaniment, so it was decided to add a humming accompaniment to the solos. I was selected to be in charge of the "humming" and I arranged it from the vocal/piano score. An old recording of a performance in 1963 was discovered a few years ago and I am listed on the cover as "director of humming". I must add that to my resume. I was very pleased when I was selected, in my senior year, to sing one of the bass solos.

We had three "literary" societies at EMC that kind of filled the role of fraternities and sororities. I was elected as President of the "Prometheans" in my junior year. This was a heady, Big Man On Campus (BMOC) position. The societies competed in drama, debates, athletics and musical events. We could perform secular music and plays—I directed and sang in a number of scenes from Gilbert and Sullivan, organized and led Barbershop quartets.

Another opportunity that increased my classical musical knowledge was my daily hour program of classical music broadcast on the campus radio station. My responsibility included selecting the music from a small library of records, researching that music to be able to air short commentary about each. This exercise informed me more than even my music history course and I received great feedback from my audience.

Many musical, religious and social opportunities presented themselves to me in my senior year. One of the most moving experiences of my life was to view J. F. Kennedy's funeral procession. We were sitting in our dorm watching the events on TV when several of us said, let's go to Washington—only about one and a half hours from EMC—and experience that historic event live. So six of us piled into a car and headed out. We got to DC around three or four o'clock in the morning, parked and chose a spot at the edge of the sidewalk where the procession would pass. I will never forget the solemnity and the awe of the crowd as the caisson moved by with only the squeaks of its wheels, the clop of the horse's hoofs, and the sight of the rider less prancing horse with an empty boot. Impressive was the sight of all the world leaders that walked in the front row of marchers behind the Kennedy family—Charles de Gaulle, Ethiopia's Haile Selassie and many I don't remember. After the procession passed, we literally ran to Arlington National Cemetery to observe the procession entering the famous cemetery and I shed some tears with the playing of Taps. As I reflect on that day, I am amazed how open it was—no medal detectors, no sniffing dogs, no checking of bags—something that couldn't happen in these days of terror and fear. There were a lot of snipers on the roofs and tons of Secret Service.

Musically, in my senior year a number of situations advanced my education. I was hired to direct a church choir in a small Presbyterian Church in a nearby town—one of the first times regularly attending a service in another church denomination let alone leading a choir. It stretched my musicianship and creativity, with only two basses and two tenors in the choir. On many Sundays one or more might be absent, and I would have to sing that part while conducting.

The organist was old and had two thumbs on each hand and two clubfeet, which added to the challenge of picking music and performing it at some respectable level. The people of the choir and congregation were truly wonderful to me. Socially, this provided for a whole new growth experience about the religious and spiritual life of non-Mennonites.

That year I also was invited to conduct the Mennonite Hour Radio Chorus. The Mennonite Hour program was broadcast from a small studio close to EMC and was aired all over the country—listened to mostly by Mennonites, but not entirely. When we finally had a radio in the house, my parents listened faithfully to it each Sunday morning before church. The chorus was a volunteer, non-auditioned group, but contained very talented singers from the Mennonite singing tradition.

We recorded two pieces for each Sunday broadcast, with rehearsals on Tuesday night. I learned the technique of choosing and rehearsing works two weeks before the broadcast—in rehearsal rotating the new pieces and polishing the pieces to be recorded that week. Luckily, a very talented musician on the staff aided in choosing much of the music. My folks were most proud of this accomplishment over all the others achieved by that time.

We recorded an album on which my mixed chorus performed six songs. This, of course, preceded the recording techniques of enhancing the sound in many ways, of great equipment and editing capabilities. We performed the works about three times in the studio and they cut the record with the best of these.

In that senior year, Earl Maust took a sabbatical to study further towards his degree and his brother, Wilbur, filled in for him. Wilbur was studying for his doctorate at the famous Indiana University, known for its great vocal department. He introduced me to better, more standard, but difficult repertoire to perform on my senior recital. I sang the entire Beethoven song cycle, *An die ferne Geliebte*, several of the old Italian arias, and several English songs—*Preach not me your musty Rules, Love in the Dictionary*, and *Love's Philosophy*. I even sang, the very difficult, Schubert *Erlkönig*, with a student accompanist—I don't know how either of us did it.

My parents, not knowing that singing a senior recital was a big deal in one's education and performing life, didn't attend, and I don't remember even being disappointed. They would have been proud, but probably wouldn't have enjoyed it. I wish I, at least, had a recording of it—I have no idea how I sounded.

Eastern Mennonite College provided a fertile atmosphere for me to develop a more encompassing view of religion, spiritual life, both personally and globally, and to continue on my spiritual evolution. My sphere of believers greatly expanded to include those from a number of different denominations and sects. The student body came mostly from conservative Mennonite homes and congregations, but the required courses in Biblical History, Mennonite history, general ethics and world religions expanded my horizons about God, salvation, Christianity, creed and doctrine.

There were just a few non-white students, but it led again to a reaffirmation of my relationships with my fellow beings. One event turned the whole campus into a discussion of race relations. We had a very talented black basketball player. Even though the sport's program did not officially participate in an intercollegiate conference, sometimes the teams traveled to play another college, usually another Christian college. On one of those trips, they were to stay overnight in a motel, but the Mennonite owner would not allow the black player to stay there. I never was so proud of my heritage as when the whole team left the motel. I just couldn't believe that a true Christian would allow such discrimination, probably for business reasons.

Fortunately, several forward thinking professors exposed me to a greater realm of Christian thought. We had to read authors, including Paul Tillich, Dietrich Bonhoefer, Soren Kierkegaard, Immanuel Kant. My view of God expanded as I read Tillich's *Ground of our Being* and J.B. Philips's *Your God is too Small*. In one class, we were required to read, J.D Salinger's *The Catcher in the Rye* with all its profanity and sex, which engendered a lively discussion.

Another spurt of spiritual growth came during the summer between my sophomore and junior years in 1962. I attended the national Mennonite youth conference in Peoria, Illinois. It gave me another step forward, advancing my understanding that devout Christians, Mennonite youth from across the country, who didn't dress like me, nor have as a restricted life, prayed just as fervently, tried to serve the Lord just as sincerely as I did.

Gradually, I got a bigger picture than the restrictive dogma of a Pennsylvania conference and congregation. Their harsh judgment of other faiths and churches was brought into conflict with what I was experiencing. On my return home, I gathered my parents in the living room and informed them of my decision to quit wearing the plain suit and change to a tradition suit coat and wear a necktie, as I didn't see that dress influenced my spiritual life at all. After a great deal of discussion and tears, they were wise enough to respect my decision. Similar events took place many, many times over the years as I progressed in my spiritual journey, for example the decision to wear wedding rings. Ironically, the son of the famous Mennonite evangelist, George R Brunk, taught me how to tie a necktie.

Dating and choosing a mate became an urgent quest as I moved toward graduation from college. Once outside of the natural gathering of young Mennonite women attending a Mennonite college, finding a suitable

partner—meaning a Mennonite—would become much more difficult. I
struggled throughout high school with asking girls for a date and it continued in college. I was very insecure, viewed myself as a "four-eyed nerd" and
was intimidated to date certain girls. However, my musical talent, revered in
the church and college alike, was my ace in the hole. My status as a student
conductor, all four years, labeled me as a leader. Leading singing, conducting
choruses, particularly the Mennonite Hour chorus, gave me a lot of visibility.

Suitable girls for marriage had to conform to my parent's church and
conference standards. Those who dressed too "worldly" for my parents were
frowned upon. "Worldly" meant that they dressed much too "liberally"—
that word having a very different context in the Pennsylvania Mennonite
Church, than of politics today. These girls wore smaller "prayer veils" at worship services, more "seductive" clothes—shorter skirts, tight straight skirts,
maybe even trousers on occasion. Their "sexy" walk and flirtation labeled
them as "loose" women.

Western Mennonite School 1964 - 66

I HAD VERY LIMITED MUSICAL goals after college graduation.   Even though I had progressed to more liberal dress and thought, experienced a non-Mennonite church, I continued to be frightened of a musical life outside the Mennonite Church. I had never experienced public school music—I student-taught at Eastern Mennonite High School situated next to the EMC campus. I really didn't think I was prepared to handle a public school teaching position. Fortunately, I didn't have to—Western Mennonite School (WMS) in Salem, Oregon hired me.

Having little traveling experience, this was an opportunity to explore an adventure I had sought for years. My longest foray from Chambersburg, Lancaster and Harrisonburg involved that trip to Florida, traveling to Ohio for my oldest brother's wedding, attending that Mennonite youth convention in Illinois and visiting my girl friend in Iowa. My mother, fearful of my going so far from home, deeply grieved and shed a lot of tears as I left for Oregon. To her it seemed I was going to the other end of the earth.

My fiancé had another year of college so I spent the first year in Oregon as a single male. I drove to Oregon from Iowa straight through with a woman who would be my colleague at WMS, in her little Volkswagen bug. Of course, it would have been inappropriate to stop at a motel—god knows what might have happened—and I didn't have the money anyway. Driving was shared, so one could attempt to sleep. The scenery was all new and fantastic to me. I remember the slow grind up some major mountains like the Big Horn and worried that we were going to be blown off the road.

At WMS, in addition to being the music teacher, I had the dubious position of Dormitory Manager (DM) in the boy's dorm, which was free rent and board, which I needed since my salary was only $2000.

I bought a small motorcycle for transportation, with a loan from a friend's father-in-law, who lived nearby—another thing that my mother did not approve of. Maybe it was that, that caused my father to make a remark about a motorcycle many years later as he was dying of cancer.

There were about 25 boys in my dorm during the week and just a handful on the weekends. I found out that there was a tradition, yes at this Christian school, of giving the Dorm Manager a very difficult time. I was a long way from home and my fiancé, which caused a sense of loneliness and separation, even though I had good friends on the faculty.

I was soon dismayed to hear that a prized tradition at WMS involved throwing the boys DM into a small stream that flowed through the campus. I determined that this showed great disrespect, was a sign of their defiance, and it wasn't going to happen to me. One very dark night, after a storm passed through, I got a whiff that this was the night. I secluded myself in my small room and locked the door. A knock came on the door, I refused to open it, so they broke it down. They forcibly picked me up, took off my glasses, which made me practically blind, and hauled me off to the stream, which due to the heavy rain was quite swollen. I kicked, screamed and, more significantly cursed, they claimed—and it probably was true. I was called on the carpet by the administration, at the request of some of the students' parents, for my bad behavior, particularly the swearing. Thankfully, some of my good new colleagues came to my defense and I was just strongly chastised.

It was odd to me that I was the one blamed for bad behavior for swearing when these Christian boys and parents saw no bad behavior in the dangerous activity of dumping the Dorm Manger in a swollen stream.

It was events like this that kept me seeking spiritually—to find my own way through the tangles of the religious, i.e. Mennonite dogma and a spiritual life. Part of my responsibilities was to lead the boys in many spiritual meetings—prayer meetings, arrange "revival" meetings, give them spiritual counseling, etc. At times, I felt as if I was faking a spiritual life with which I was becoming increasingly uncomfortable.

My musical development continued to evolve even as I taught. The music program at WMS centered on a small, auditioned choir that went on a long tour each spring, partly as a recruitment tool for the school. We sang in Mennonite churches and stayed in the homes of their members. As director, I was often requested to stay at the minister's home. I was so young and baby-faced that when I stepped off of the bus, I was asked where the director was.

We sang all sacred music from a wide variety of genre, motets, parts of oratorios, spirituals, and ethnic music, using a lot of the repertoire from my college experience. The small group trained from childhood in the art of four-part a cappella singing, performed at a quite high standard.

The tours were great adventures for me, extending over 2000 miles each year. The first year, spring of 1965, we toured south, through southern Oregon, Idaho, Wyoming into southern Colorado. The second year, we toured north, through Eastern Oregon, into northern Idaho, North Dakota, up through Saskatchewan, Canada, west through Alberta and British Colombia, south through Washington to Oregon. In Alberta, we traveled far north approaching the Yukon Territory to sing at a small Mennonite Mission Church in Eaglesham, that was the home of one of our choir members. The spring mud season had set in and the driver of the big bus had a "fun" time negotiating the last 50 miles or so, on a dirt, "mud" road.

The next year 1965-66, I signed up for one more year at WMS. I was married in the summer of 1965, and my wife acquired a position as math teacher at WMS and we traveled the entire way across the country on a borrowed credit card from my brother—I don't know how we signed it—and a pup tent in my 1964 Plymouth Valiant.

Without the Dorm Manager position, I really enjoyed that year. We lived in a small house trailer, loaned to us by a faculty member on sabbatical. It was parked on the property of a Mennonite owned farm, close to the school. The trailer had recently been moved there, so I had to dig a septic pit, by hand. We used the farmer's freezer to preserve vegetables from their gardens and the wonderful Oregon fruit—peaches, raspberries and the great boysenberries from the Willamette Valley. With a frozen quarter of beef, fresh eggs and slaughtered chickens from our farmer, our weekly grocery budget was $5.00. Now that we had two salaries, mine upped to $2200 and my wife's $2000, we sent money back to my Dad, to repay his loan to buy the Plymouth, and we still lived pretty well.

While at WMS, in the spring of 1966, I was hired for my first professional gig. Seeing an announcement of auditions, for the bass solo roles in the "*Messiah*" in a performance in Albany, Oregon, I signed up with great trepidation, as well as a curious anticipation. I hadn't sung those solos publically but studied hard, practicing them with an old pump organ left in our little trailer. Unexpectedly—the old impostor syndrome—they engaged me and I got paid very little, but I was proud that someone actually hired me. It was the first time I felt that I really deserved a role, because at Eastern Mennonite, I had been a big fish in a small pond.

Since EMC didn't have any instruments on campus, we didn't have instrumental methods courses, courses that introduce you, minimally, to the brass, strings, woodwinds and percussion families. So, I signed up for Brass Methods one semester and Woodwind Methods the second semester at Willamette University, a very respected school, in Salem, just about 20 minutes from Western Mennonite School.

For each instrumental family, you chose one for more concentrated study. I enjoyed playing the clarinet and concentrated on that for the woodwind class. Even though, we had no instrumental teacher at WMS, a number of the students were studying instruments, with lessons in their home communities. To give them an incentive to continue to study and to give them a group experience, I informally formed a small chamber ensemble. I think we had a violin, flute, oboe and my clarinet. However, I only embarrassed myself, and probably the students as I squeaked though the entire program. I bowed out of the ensemble for the future. In the brass class at Willamette, I enjoyed the trumpet, bought one, took lessons in graduate school for a year or two—but dropped them when I didn't have the time to practice.

Graduate School 1966 - 1970

AFTER TEACHING HIGH SCHOOL FOR two years, my desire for further learning of the wide world of music kicked in and I decided to attend graduate school. However, that meant taking the scary step of the unknown—attending a secular university, competing in a real music program. Could I cut it? What would the atmosphere be like? I decided to apply to schools close to one of our parents, the University of Iowa, near my wife's home and Temple University in Philadelphia, somewhat near my parent's home. My wife applied for teaching positions in both areas and, if I were accepted at both, her obtaining a job would determine the school.

Her first offer came from the high school in West Branch, Iowa, about 15 minutes from the University. We lived that first year in the quaint little village—home of Herbert Hoover—in a nice basement apartment owned by a generous older couple, thinking that my wife would have more school activities than I would. But, it was just the opposite; I had increasing activities in the Music Department, more rehearsals and concerts in the evenings and weekends, so the next year we moved into an apartment in Iowa City where the University was located.

The third and fourth year we took a further step to decrease our rent bill. Some of the student housing for married students were old military barracks. The outside was covered with corrugated metal and the inside very plain with concrete floors. But the rent was $65 a month with all utilities. With that savings we put in an inexpensive carpet, a window air conditioner, bought an old upright piano and a new Dodge Charger. I erected a picket fence around our little yard to make it even homier.

On our arrival to the area, we joined the First Mennonite Church of Iowa City, and became involved in activities there. In the second year, I became Choir Director

I also sang as a soloist in the First Baptist Church service, where my best friend in the Iowa music department, was choir director. Its service was 9:00-10:00 and the Mennonite service began at 11:00, so I was able to hustle over in time for the choir duties. We collaborated on a number of projects with small instrumental ensembles—the Fauré Requiem and a Bach Cantata. I sang the bass solos at First Baptist while he conducted and I conducted at First Mennonite and he sang the bass solos.

My best friend and his wife were the first non-Mennonites that we invited over for dinner. We didn't know them very well, but knew they were Christian, but I still remember the angst surrounding that event—do we serve wine, do we say a grace before the meal, what do we talk about. It went so well that consequently we relaxed in those situations.

At First Mennonite there were quite a few young married couples, some with small families and with similar backgrounds, attending graduate school. Four of us couples decided to form a small group—to spend time together not just socially but to also discuss various books and topics relevant to current events. These discussions presented the opportunity for me to adjust, grow and evolve further on my spiritual journey. One that was not defined by "dos and don'ts" but a value system, a moral code, a way of life guided by the principles set out in the Bible, Jesus and other sources.

Most of our social life centered on these Mennonite friends. We did a number of things together including each couple buying a ticket to the Iowa football games, another new adventure, which I really enjoyed. Although the temperature was brutally cold, we layered up with clothes and had big thermoses of coffee—actually coffee.

At the Sunday service, we graduate students formed a Sunday school class—we called Witmarsum, after the town where Menno Simons, the founder of the Mennonites lived. We tackled some complex issues of our spiritual life, challenged some of our inherited beliefs, explored all phases of spiritually by reading the Bible as a guidepost, rather than the literal translation of my youth and books like Joseph Fletcher's *Situational Ethics,* John Yoder's *The Politics of Jesus.*

Not viewing myself as an intellect, I was quite surprised to be chosen as a co-leader of this group. I dived wholeheartedly into this study, because it was fascinating and inspiring to me. The discussions, and my preparations to lead them, stretched my image of God, of the divinity of Jesus, the meaning of morality, and the political implications of my faith.

My conference of Mennonites believed in "non-resistance". To us war was always wrong—there was no such thing as a "just" war. But our discussions at Witmarsum seriously questioned that. For example, Dietrich Bonheoffer became involved in a movement to assassinate Hitler, but died regretting that decision and asking God for forgiveness.

The ministers of both churches were quite liberal thinking, theologically, and very aware of world affairs—the Vietnam War with protests, the Kent State killings, and the draft. They were very skillful in blending together a service of hymns, Bible readings, poetry and a homily of current events and a Christian response to it.

The government allowed Mennonites and Quakers—called peace churches—to have conscientious objector status. They allowed us to serve "alternative service" for two years rather than serving in the military. Young men who were drafted served in positions with the park service, hospitals of all kinds, teaching positions in Mennonite schools and more.

I was always one step ahead of the draft as requirements changed—e.g. I was married, then I was a graduate student, then I had a child. I panicked about halfway through my planned graduate program when I received a IO status, which meant that I was in the lottery pool and if my number came up, I would have to interrupt my studies and serve my two years of alternative service. I was ashamed, however, when I realized that there were many "conscientious objectors" who were denied IO classification because they weren't members of a traditionally peace denomination.

With their IA classification, if called, they would be required to serve in the military.

My musical experience before graduate school was grossly inadequate compared to my peers who graduated from prestigious schools, such as, St Olaf, Oberlin, Concordia and other excellent universities. I kept my mouth shut and my ears and eyes on full alert. I spent hours and hours in the Music Listening Library listening to works that I knew nothing about, but were discussed in classes and in casual conversation with fellow students and friends. I needed to become acquainted with the names of singers, operas, orchestras, conductors, art songs, Masses, oratorios to be up to speed at the graduate level.

Everything I was learning interested and challenged me. I was so thrilled by every new discovery that encouraged me to keep seeking. A thorough study of music history explained a great deal of the great composers and their works, of various music periods of composition, which I had only peripherally studied at Eastern Mennonite. I knew little about analysis of music and was amazed at the structure of music as well as the aesthetic of music. I learned about vocal pedagogy, vocal diction, and art song literature.

I attended many orchestral, chamber music, solo instrumental recitals, to make up for my lack to knowledge of these genres. Several years, I traveled to Minneapolis to hear the Metropolitan Opera touring company, hearing great singers like Richard Tucker, Franco Corelli, Renata Tebaldi, Regine Crespin—where we got the idea to name our daughter, Regina--Robert Merrill, and many more. Twice, I attended performances by the great Lieder singer, Dietrich Fischer Dieskau, at the Chicago Symphony Hall. For the first time, I heard many of the great choral works at the University. These years of growth gave me new ideals, goals, ambitions, and deeper perspectives.

I began my studies at Iowa as a choral major, not a voice major, which meant I was looking to become a better choir director, instead of a solo singer. I sang in the select chamber choir, enjoying new repertoire that was more modern, more difficult, and much of it secular.

But the highlight of that first year was singing the Giuseppe Verdi *Requiem* with a chorus of some 150 singers, a full orchestra and our esteemed voice faculty as soloists. It was an astounding moment for me, an exciting, invigorating, ear popping musical and spiritual experience. It was an "I thought I had died and gone to Heaven" moment. I had never heard such wonderful solo singing and I had never sung with an orchestra or a chorus of so many talented voices. To top it off, several of us graduate students were hired a few weeks later by Grinnell College, to be ringers in their performance of the *Requiem*. I never dreamed that I would conduct it three times in my lifetime.

Being a choral music major, I was assigned to a graduate assistant for my weekly voice lessons. He was a very good teacher and early in the semester, impressed with my voice and my vocal progress, he made the comment that I needed to study with a full faculty member and he recommended his teacher, Albert Gammon. I was, of course, flattered and thrilled, but greatly intimidated.

Mr. Gammon was a very tall, elegant man with a huge bass voice, who amazed me at his solo performance of the Verdi Requiem. He spoke with very proper English diction. What a wonderful, generous man! Mr. Gammon became not only my voice teacher, but my advocate, my mentor, and after I graduated, my friend. I owe so much to him, for changing my life and leading me into the career that I couldn't dream of. Music which fed my soul, enhanced my passion, was inseparable from my spiritual life, became my career,

Mr. Gammon and I talked on the phone numerous times over the years, and when I found that he was dying of cancer, I called him and had the opportunity to tell him what he meant to me and what he gave me. His last words to me were "Carroll, you know I have always loved you." Mr. Gammon, I still think of you often and pass on many things that you taught me to my students.

I became increasingly aware of my developing vocal skills, liked the literature and enjoyed solo performing, so decided to major in vocal performance. I fell in love with opera very quickly. I had only seen a bad film version of the opera, *La Boheme* by Puccini, before the summer of 1966. That summer, before beginning my studies at the University, I attended their opera production of Mozart's *Cosi van tutte*. Oh, how I loved it and said I would love to participate in an opera, even just carrying a third spear, not knowing that I would sing the lead role of Guglielmo many years later.

I enrolled in the opera workshop and sang in the chorus of several productions. Soon I was thrust into small principle roles, Fiorello in Rossini's *The Barber of Seville*, Dr. Blind in Johann Strauss's *Die Fledermaus*. I had never acted before, except in a couple of skits in college. I had never taken an acting class; I had never been on stage. I had to learn the skills in performing opera on the fly.

Thankfully, I had several excellent and patient stage directors who led me through the learning of stagecraft. I had to learn directions such as downstage, upstage, props, stage right, stage left, etc. I was totally amazed that I was chosen, through auditions, to sing the lead roles of Jupiter in Offenbach's *Jupiter in the Underworld*, Germont in Verdi's *La Traviata* and Figaro in Mozart's *Le Nozze di Figaro*. Singing Germont was again a "died and gone to heaven" moment. The beginning of Act II, with his conversation with the courtesan, Violetta, imploring her to leave his son, whom she loved dearly, remains very close to my heart.

Receiving a number of kind reviews in local newspapers, encouraged me:

Orpheus in the Underworld
    "The show-stopper was Carroll Lehman, as the inept, but resourceful Jupiter"
The Marriage of Figaro
    "Figaro, performed by Carroll Lehman was presented as a sincere, friendly and clever chap. The audience laughed and applauded enthusiastically"

With the opera workshop, I entered into a world I knew nothing about, a truly secular environment. I had never heard women swear like sailors, or flirt so obviously. Rumors abounded about who was doing whom. There were many not so secret affairs and trysts occurring among the students. It was rumored that I was sleeping with my Susannah in Figaro because we car-pooled to rehearsals.

It was in this context that I learned more about gay men and women and their life styles. I don't ever remember having a prejudice against gays, but never really had the opportunity to associate with them in my youth. Many people were still not out of the closet, but people knew.

Our opera performance space was a small auditorium in a former state capital building. There were no dressing rooms, so we used a hallway on the second floor behind the stage. An imaginary line separated the men's and the women's dressing space. Only a limited amount of modesty was possible, as people were running around in their underwear and bras while putting on make-up and costumes. I had to learn to just deal.

Although I was focused on my vocal studies, I aspired to be a conductor, specifically of works with orchestra. I worked diligently in conducting class, consciously observed conductors of all types and was determined to learn from the orchestra conductor, James Dixon, who was superb and a protégé of the great Minneapolis Symphony conductor, Dimitri Metropoulis. Dixon was a taskmaster: took no prisoners, but was a very clear and precise conductor. I decided that I would seek to be a complete conductor, not just a "choral" conductor.

The choral conductor at Iowa was a well-respected director on the choral scene nationally, but the fine orchestra members did not respect him as a well-rounded conductor with a clear technique. When he conducted the large choral masterworks, like the Verdi *Requiem*, the players would cross their legs and intentionally play poorly to embarrass him.

Mr. Dixon team-taught the graduate conducting class with the choral conductor. It was Dixon's insights and instructions that served me the best when I conducted. I sang a number of my operas under his baton and learned by listening and watching. Over the years, I was most proud of compliments, particularly from the professional soloists and orchestra members, about the clarity of my conducting and my knowledge of the works, musically and emotionally.

In 1969, my last year at Iowa, my son was born. The Lamaze Method of natural childbirth was new and I particularly liked that husbands were allowed in the delivery room, if you took a Lamaze class. I wanted to be a part of my child's birth as much as a man could. I didn't want to be deprived of this great life experience. A friend of mine was the first man to be allowed in the delivery room at University Hospital in Iowa City. I was the second. It was a awesome experience—everything I thought it would be.

It was July 20th 1969, the day that the first man stepped out onto the moon. I went from the delivery room, when nothing was happening, to a lounge to watch TV. After his birth, I went home, had a couple drinks, and watch Neil Armstrong descend from the lander onto the moon surface. Scott was about six weeks premature and suffered from Hyaline Membrane, a potentially fatal condition of the lungs. Fluid remains in the lungs and unless the infant can expel it, he will not survive. There is nothing that can be done about it, and the agony of waiting was hell.

I was singing a lead role in the summer opera that was composed by a member of the Iowa music faculty, entitled *Four Thousand Dollars*. It was a challenge to visit Scott in the hospital, weep by his incubator, compose myself and truck off to sing a damn opera I didn't like. It was not a very good composition and I did not enjoy performing it.

The opera was about a logging camp and the loggers spent a lot of time playing poker. As mentioned, I had never played with real cards, since it was a Mennonite no-no. Several others of the cast had never played poker, as well, so we would show up for rehearsal about a half hour early and play penny poker in order to be proficient enough not to distract us when singing while dealing, betting, etc. We literally sang, while dealing: "A Jack, a Queen, Two ladies", and such phrases as "I check", "you're bluffing, "I call" and many other poker terms.

While in Iowa City, I learned more about my wife's family, who were Amish until she was ten. Her parents were still very conservative Mennonites, but his Amish brothers "shunned" her father when he left the Amish church. My wife told stories of family gatherings that were very painful—Amish siblings sat a one end of the table and non-Amish sat at the other and didn't speak to each other.

She still had many Amish cousins in the area and I was curious of the Amish service, and what music was presented. My wife arranged for one of her cousins to take us by horse and buggy to a Sunday morning service. What a fascinating experience. This is as close to experiencing life a century ago as one can get. Sitting in a canvas buggy, listening to the crunch of the big wheels on the dirt road—Iowa still had quite a few of them in 1968—the clip clop of the horse's hoofs, the slow drift of the scenery going by, were awe inspiring. It was beautiful.

The service was, as usual, held in the barn of a church member. The buggies were unhitched, parked and the men took their horses to a corral. The women went about planning and organizing the meal, provided after the service—potluck.

The actual service lasted about four hours, with a lot of singing, long prayers and a sermon. The backless benches became very hard as the time went by. The entire service was in one of two kinds of German. The hymns, sermon and prayers were in "low" German, sometimes called "Pennsylvania Dutch", even in Iowa. The Bible was read in "Hoch Deutch"—High German—spoken mainly in Northern Germany. The hymns were long, drawn out events, much sliding and slurry between very long held notes, sung in four parts, and sometimes in unison, much like Gregorian chant.

The Amish people were very kind and friendly to us. At the meal I spent quite a bit of time making conversation about farms, horses, crops, etc—which I could do, given my upbringing. It was not nearly as awkward as I thought it would be.

I can't over emphasize what those four years in Iowa City, 1966 – 1970, meant to my growth—musically, educationally, spiritually, and personally. But, I looked forward to a new phase of my life, of finally diving into the real world, to spread my wings, to further reach for some of my goals and aspirations. And with some anxiety, I left the cocoon of Iowa City, the University, the First Mennonite Church, the Baptist church and our little group of families.

Hope College 1970 - 1975

By the spring of 1970, I had completed all of my requirements for the Doctor of Musical Arts in Vocal Literature and Pedagogy, except for the two required recitals and the doctoral thesis.

I applied to many colleges for positions of teaching voice and associated classes. Most of my friends received job offers and headed off to their prospective new experiences, leaving me behind feeling a little nervous and sorry for myself. We could stay another year and really finish the degree, but it was time for me to get a college position and finish the degree requirements while teaching. Fairly late in the summer, I saw an opening at Hope College in Holland, Michigan. I researched it to find that it was a liberal arts college affiliated with the Dutch Reformed Church of America. It had a great reputation in general and music specifically. The city of Holland was located on the Lake Macatawa, which connected to Lake Michigan by a man-made channel. I quickly applied and "hoped" for the best.

In August, I received an invitation for an interview and audition. We had no money for lodging amenities, but I wanted my wife to accompany me, so we packed our pup tent, our little Scott and headed to Holland for the interview. We camped at a great little park right on Lake Michigan, next to the channel that went into Lake Macatawa. I loved the setting and I really wanted this job.

While I was being interviewed, my wife was pushing Scott around the campus in a stroller. The interview went well, I liked the people and they seemed to like me, and I thought I sang well. They saw on my vita that I had some conducting experience, but they informed me, very clearly, that there would be no choral group for me to conduct. That was a disappointment, but not enough to turn down a wonderful position.

Holland is a beautiful town, founded by Dutch immigrants. I was impressed that there were about 50 churches in the city, somewhat equally divided between the Dutch Reformed Church of America, and the Christian Reformed Church of America, the latter being much more conservative. And there was representation of most other Christian denominations, but no Mennonite church. I was told, after I got the job, that two things were in my favor—I was Mennonite, and my wife strolling around the campus with our young son impressed them.

Since I was hired in August, we didn't have a lot of time to buy a house, which we really wanted to do. We rented a summer cabin near the Macatawa while we shopped. We found and bought a very nice smaller house in the center of Holland with a nice yard, that we fenced to protect our kids and our new collie puppy, from the street. In the corner of the beautiful lawn I started a flower garden and even planted a few greens.

Moving to Holland meant moving away from a Mennonite community. As mentioned, the city was heavily populated with churches, but no Mennonites. We attended a few churches, but were not satisfied with any one. My experiences of searching, discussing questioning faith and religion, in Iowa City, led me to be somewhat cynical of institutional religion. I struggled with many of the platitudes in the church services, with the rituals, and of the lingo of the leaders. I continued on a more personal journey—seeking my inner spirit, a changing idea of God and concentrating on my relationship to my fellow human beings.

For some extra bucks, I filled in at times as choir director—in a Dutch Reformed Church and a Presbyterian Church—but never, really, affiliated with one church with regular attendance.

I couldn't have asked for a better first teaching position. Hope College is a truly liberal arts college with very talented students, many interested in music, even though it might not be their major. We had a superb, widely known touring choir, a Vespers choir of mainly underclassmen and those who couldn't pass an audition into the touring choir. There was a Collegium Musicum, a small group that specialized in performing early music. A fine symphonic orchestra of all student musicians performed some of the great orchestral literature and an even smaller, more select symphonette that was auditioned from the larger orchestra. This ensemble was the touring instrumental arm of the college.

I taught about 18 private voice students, a general music class, started an opera workshop, and taught vocal diction. In the second or third year, the director of the Collegium went on a sabbatical and I was asked to fill his position. The music department chair and others were impressed with my choral abilities and when another of our faculty members went on sabbatical, I was given the large Vespers chorus to conduct. When he returned, he wanted me to continue. I directed it until I left Hope in 1975. A year after acquiring that position, I decided to morph it into an oratorio chorus, performing works with our symphonic orchestra.

For our first such collaboration, I chose the Vivaldi *Gloria*, a fairly simple work, using a small Baroque orchestra and with few conducting difficulties. My parents came out to hear it. My mother's comments were: "Why do you have to use an orchestra?" It would be so much better a cappella" and "Why do you have to sing it in Latin"?

Now I desired the opportunity to attempt conducting a work with a large orchestra. I asked the orchestra conductor, to share a concert with the oratorio chorus. We chose the Johannes Brahms' *Schicksalslied* and Howard Hanson's *Song of Democracy*. He rehearsed the orchestra and I the oratorio chorus for both works. We decided I would conduct the Brahms and he the Hanson. I was totally intimidated by the large excellent student orchestra. I diligently studied the score so that I was in complete command of it.

I felt the need to continue to study voice, privately. A very successful teacher in Chicago, Hermanus Baer, was recommended to me. His greatest student at the time was Sherrill Milnes, an international baritone who a admired greatly and had his voice on a number of recordings. It was the first time out of the cradle of my dear teacher at Iowa, Albert Gammon. I drove to Chicago for these lessons every couple of weeks and I learned a great deal from his teachings. I would often stay for an opera or concert in Chicago to continue my exposure to the great literature of music.

While at Hope I remained active as a solo performer. I presented both of my doctoral recitals on the faculty recital series and then performed them at Iowa. Hope pianist faculty member, Anthony Kooiker, a superb pianist and coach, accompanied me. He had been an accompanist for some years for a rising violinist, Albert Spaulding, who died very young and Tony went into academia. Tony, a lover of opera and art song, and very experienced in playing both, taught me a immensely in my preparation of those required doctoral recitals.

I had always wanted to sing the title role in Mendelssohn's oratorio, *Elijah*. I asked the orchestra conductor if he would be willing to conduct the performance—I would prepare the choir and sing the title role. The orchestra performed at a high level; we hired some other fine soloists and it was a booming success. The *Holland Sentinel* review wrote of Lehman's excellent portrayal of the prophet.

In a collaboration of the music and theatre departments, we performed the John Gay's *Beggar's Opera*. The chair of our department and reprised the role of Peachem. I also performed my first professional opera role. A small theatre company out of Grand Rapids decided to perform Puccini's *Gianni Schicchi*. I auditioned and was hired to sing the role of Simone, one of the biggest roles other than the title role of Schicchi.

I sang Bach's solo cantata, *Ich habe genug*, on a ten-day tour with the Hope College symphonette. A funny anecdote: we performed mostly in Dutch Reformed Churches and, since we were the tour VIPs, we were invited to stay at the pastors' homes. Of course, most of them didn't drink and after a concert the conductor and I would like a nip or two. We had stashed a flask of whiskey in our suitcases, so when we excused ourselves and went to bed, we imbibed.

One of the most difficult performances on that tour was a Sunday church service in Denver, the mile high city, at 10:00 a.m. We had just arrived the night before, so little time to acclimate to the high altitude. I had to draw on all my skills of breath control and vocal technique to manage an acceptable performance. All of these experiences gave me an immense growth spurt from a graduate student to a professional singer and college professor.

During time at Hope, I was privileged to teach a number of very talented students, some who went on to teaching and/or advanced degrees. I taught a number of very talented theatre majors who established acting careers. The most successful was Daytime Emmy award winner, Kim Zimmer, who became famous, mostly as a long time regular on the soap opera "The Guiding Light" as the character, Riva. Hope College gave me the opportunity to continue to improve in the art of teaching and, particularly, the teaching of voice at a college level.

I suffered my first panic attack while at Hope and only in my 30s. One day in the studio, I felt short of breath, some discomfort in my chest, and with all the history of my father's heart disease, I assumed I was having a heart event. I called my wife and she quickly drove me the couple of blocks to the hospital. They thoroughly checked me out and concluded that I wasn't having a heart event, but kept me in the hospital overnight. In those days the words, "panic/anxiety attack" weren't in the medical vocabulary. They didn't say it, of course, but I felt they thought I was a hypochondriac and I was embarrassed. That was the first of many panic attacks over my life—but mostly spared of them for several years now. They are now recognized as a real and honest phenomenon.

With a very busy schedule, I tried to interject researching and writing on my doctoral essay, even though I had mixed feelings about it. I really thought it wasn't necessary for me to receive the doctoral degree. I learned so many practical things in graduate school—how to become a better musician, a good balanced singer, vocal pedagogy and literature--and didn't feel that writing a doctoral thesis would add to that education. But, wiser people told me I would regret not finishing it since I was so close, that I would not get tenure or a position at another college without it.

So, I buckled down and wrote the damn thesis: *Benjamin Carr: his contribution to early American solo vocal literature.* I did enjoy the historical research, finding his works in many libraries, such as London, Library of Congress and the Free Library of Philadelphia. I received copies of his songs by correspondence; however, a highlight of my research was a trip to Philadelphia to see some of his original letters in the rare book collection. They allowed me to enter the sacred archives and brought the letters to me to read and then they copied them for me and I included them in my thesis. I was thrilled to hold the old onionskin letters written by Benjamin Carr in 1794.

I often think how different a task the writing of that thesis would have been, with computers—like I am using now. As we were taught in those days, I put all my research notes on four by five cards, organized them into a logical order and wrote my first draft by hand on yellow legal pads. I did a quick edit and my wife typed a first draft. I asked several good writers on the Hope faculty to edit it, had another draft typed and sent it to key members of my committee at the University. They penciled in their comments and sent it back, often disagreeing among themselves. Another draft was typed and I was ready to defend it to the entire committee at my oral exam.

Since most of the committee members had a hand in the written product, the exam went well. One committee member, a voice teacher who didn't view himself as an academician was honest and said that he hadn't read it and would let the rest of the committee decide. After passing the exam and making the corrections, I hired a professional typist, who knew the picky University requirements for margins, heading, fonts, etc. I didn't want the damn thing rejected by the graduate school for an improper format.

I regarded the pomp and circumstance of graduation a bunch of hooey, and didn't attend. I received my diploma through the mail and I've lived to regret that decision a bit, because I worked so hard to earn it and I should have been proud to walk across the stage to receive it. Later, it became obvious that it was a wise decision to actually get the degree. As predicted, I would not have gotten a full-time, tenure track position at an acceptable college without it.

In 1971, my daughter, Regina, was born. I sought the privilege of being in the delivery room and watching that miracle of life happen again. We had a superb doctor who was liberal and knowledgeable about the trends in child birthing. No husband had ever been allowed in the delivery room at the Holland Hospital, but I pleaded with the Doctor to allow me to be there, since I had been there for my son's birth, I had a track record of not freaking out or being a pain in the ass.

He said he would try to honor my request, but couldn't promise since that was not the current policy of the hospital. Only as he was going down the hall to the delivery room, did he throw me surgical scrubs and said, "Come on" with a grin on his face. How wonderful to see the head pop out and that she had red hair, a trait that appeared once in a while on both sides of my family. But, she had a bit of a difficulty—she had the cord wrapped around her neck, so they had to work fast to disengage it. She was a bit jaundiced, also, and needed to be in an incubator for a couple of days.

Holland offered me the opportunity to experience my love of the water, just walking out on the pier that led to an old historic lighthouse, to go to a beach a dusk. I began to fish in Lake Michigan, just from the pier. I mainly caught perch on a rod and would net for smelt, a very small, but tasty fish that my family learned to enjoy.

I had a professor friend who was a big fisherman—he lived to fish. One summer he invited us to visit them in a rented cabin where they were staying for a couple of weeks. It was on a relatively small lake, but he said there was some wonderful fishing out there. He supplied the small boat, all the fishing gear and lots of kind advice. We weren't fishing very long, when I had something bite and I was able to hook it and he knew it was something big. It was a seven-pound lake trout, which I guess was quite large for that small lake. He was more excited than I was, took his line in and steered the boat around to make it possible for me to land this "monster".

We were leaving that day so, he instructed us to freeze it in water and take it home. When my parents and a couple friends stopped in Holland to visit, I pulled out this fish to bake for them. A friend gave me a Mexican glaze to put on it and it came out of the oven, golden. I wanted to put the whole fish on a large platter and bring it to the table, but Mom said that I couldn't: " I'm not having those eyes look up at me". To this day, I remember it as one of the best fish I ever have tasted. Maybe a bit biased.

While living in Holland and seeking an active intellectual life as well as a social life, similar to what we had in Iowa City, we became a part of a faculty book club of young faculty with diverse spiritual beliefs from an atheist to a person on the Bible faculty. We discussed many different genres of books, not just spiritual ones. In addition, two families moved in across the street—the men were seminary students at the Dutch Reformed Seminary next to the college. We were about the same age and with a similar inquisitiveness about life.

These two groups aided in my transitioning from the group at the Iowa City Mennonite Church to a community of spiritual, but not necessarily Christian or religious people, all seeking life and its meaning. We discussed morals, ethics, civic responsibility, and much more, outside the context of a religion, the Bible, a denomination or an ethnic group—Jew, Christian, Protestant or Catholic. In that context, I continued to grow and modify my spiritual life that came from my Mennonite heritage. I was breaking from the burden of guilt, the literalness of Bible, the concept of Heaven and Hell to, what seemed to me, a more healthy approach of having a spiritual compass of one's own, originating in many beliefs.

As one of my professors, way back at Eastern Mennonite College, said that in a lot of religions, God is a God of Judgment, but Mennonites believed in a God of Love. It seemed incongruous to me at the time, with all the judgment that descended from my Mennonite church life.

Europe 1972

As I STUDIED MUSIC AND, particularly, Western vocal and choral music, I craved an opportunity to visit Europe and put a context to these works, the composers and cultures. In 1972, I applied for and received a grant from Hope College to study German for a month in a very concentrated program at a Goethe Institute. I did some research and found one in a small town in Bavaria--Kochel am See. Goethe Institutes are located all around the world. I could have attended one in Boston or Chicago, but wanted to be immersed in the culture and language by living in the country.

Scott was almost three and Regina was about to have her first birthday in June. So, we decided to take Scott along and my sister-in-law, Mary Louise and brother, Wilmer, took Gina for the six weeks we were gone. Gina celebrated her first birthday with them, and she never lets me forget it.

We flew out on May 29, which meant I experienced my thirtieth birthday on the way to Europe. We flew into Paris to visit some friends, a couple that we knew in college and graduate school. He had a Fulbright Grant to study and teach in a school in Paris. He had received his PhD in French from Iowa. They were one of the families in our little study group. We didn't have a lot of money for nice hotels, so we tented just outside of Paris with them in a campground—real romantic.

On the way there from the airport a policeman in a small town stopped us for some irregularity of the license plate on the rented car. When he checked our friend's visa, the policeman didn't understand a Fulbright scholar and declared that our friend didn't have the proper visa to stay in France. Of course, my wife and I didn't know what he was saying, but thank god our friend was fluent in French. The policeman hauled us into the little town, took our friend before the magistrate, while we sat in the car confused and a bit scared of being at the mercy of some little town judge. After a few phone calls to American consulate, they allowed us to proceed.

After Paris, we traveled by train to Kochel and settled into a very small space—here we would call it a studio apartment—in the house of a family in the center of the small village. I studied for four weeks--six hours on Monday, Wednesday and Friday and four hours on Tuesday and Thursday. But, when I walked downtown I couldn't understand the people. How could I not be learning German well enough to speak to the local folks? It wasn't until I met some Northern Germans, and I could understand them quite well and they could understand me, that I realized we were learning "Hoch" Deutsch—high German—and it was very different than the heavy accents of the Bavarians in Kochel. The southern Germans have an accent like Texans or Georgians have here—much more of a draw and a flat sound to their speech.

After the Institute, we rented a car and traveled across Austria into Italy for about two weeks. We wanted to visit the highlights of Salzburg, Venice, Florence and Rome.

We had a number of interesting coincidences in our travels. We went to the Paris Opera House to see a performance, and looking down from the second floor onto the lobby below, we saw a graduate school colleague.

When we arrived in Zurich, I remembered that an old friend from University of Iowa, a student I had sung opera with, was engaged as a singer at the Opera House. We walked down to the House just to observe and saw on a poster that she was singing Gilda in Verdi's opera, *Rigoletto,* that night and decided to buy one ticket, so that one of us could stay with Scott while the other went to the opera. I went to Act I, and then rushed to our nearby hotel and my wife went to the second Act and I then went to the third Act.

In Venice, we saw that an American Choral Directors' Conference was being held in the city and fortunately a group of them were performing a concert in St. Mark's Cathedral that afternoon. The great composer, Giovanni Gabrieli, developed what became to be known as the "Venetian school" of composition. His works were mostly polychoral—meaning several choruses. They were to be performed antiphonally and were most famous for being performed in St. Marks with various groups of musicians performing from the different balconies. It was a thrill to sit in the center of the cathedral and hear the antiphony of groups on balconies on the left and on the right, small brass ensembles from the another, vocal soloist from some of the pulpits jaunting out from an inner wall—live surround sound music. I thought I recognized someone in one of the choirs and, sure enough, it was one of my professors at Iowa.

When we planned our trip, we wondered how having a two-year old child with us would work. But it went very well, if we were attentive to his needs. We learned that we had to remember his naptime and plan for something that would aid in his falling asleep. It could be something like sitting at a café while he, with his "bankie" laid beside us, or taking an extended tram ride, or sitting on a park bench. If we didn't do this, we paid.

We discovered that children are an opener to connecting with people. People of all countries love a child. Scott was an icebreaker in many situations. For instance, when we got to Florence, inexpensive housing—a pension—was at a premium and we were worried about being able to find one. We walked up to one, that we found in our travel book, knocked on the door and the lady said in broken English that she had no room, but then she spied Scott and gushed, "a Bambino" and reached to pick him up. She not only had a room, but she and her teenage daughter adopted Scott. They asked to be able to take him in to their part of the house and we trusted them enough to let them babysit him while we went out to dinner, alone.

We didn't make it to Rome; our travel ended in Florence. We got a telegram saying that my mother-in-law had died. We went to the American Express office and they took care of all the arrangements for us to fly home the next morning. I remained a loyal member of American Express for many years. Our arranged flight didn't leave until evening so, we still had some time to explore Florence—we went to the Uffizi Gallery and then to see Michelangelo's sculpture of David. The reproductions of him are nothing like the real one, overwhelming in size, glistening in the bright, natural lighting, showing every ripple of muscle that Michelangelo so carefully had studied and reproduced. The emotion of the news and seeing this magnificent creation brought forth the tears.

That trip was an immense education for this Mennonite farm boy's development. It was captivating to see all the old history in those countries, to see the cathedrals, the artwork, the mountains and the origins of music I had studied and performed.

Bellingham, Washington
1975-1978

THE NEXT PHASE OF MY life took a very different turn from anything that I had experienced before, and caused some of the greatest pain that I would emotionally experience in life.

I was growing restless and weary of academia—I had been in it most of my life—twenty years of study and seven years of teaching. I was tired of the stress, the political bullshit from administration, to the responsibility of the rules and regulations of tenure, evaluation reports, budgets and the religious restriction of parochial institutions like Western Mennonite School and Hope College.

Being an idealist got me in trouble, sometimes, with the status quo. Joining in protest marches, arguing for reasonable rules for students, not being a member of a specific church was not looked upon kindly by Hope College community.

With the two families living across the street, we often discussed the advantages of a community of people, living on the same property, in a communal lifestyle of sharing common means of living—of living off the land, and decision making by consensus. One couple traveled around the country to search for a property that was affordable, was large enough to accommodate and sustain a number of families. In 1973, they found a hundred acre farm outside of Bellingham, Washington, near the small town of Everson.

Its buildings were in really bad condition, but it was a beautiful plot of land, looking toward the Cascades with a magnificent view of Mt. Baker. On good clear, cool days it felt like you could reach out and touch it. The two families were joined by a third, whom they had befriended, and they bought the farm.

They rented the carriage house of a wonderful estate in Bellingham while they fixed up the buildings at the farm—barely enough to live in. We traveled to visit them in summer of 1974, to see if we would want to try this lifestyle. We stayed in the estate house, a magnificent building with a beautiful view of the city. It had a great hall that was surrounded by a balcony overlooking—the bedrooms opening into that balcony. Having just read the F. Scott Fitzgerald's novel, *The Great Gatsby*, I envisioned a room full of dancers in the great hall with people holding champagne glasses, men in tuxedos and women in glorious gowns.

While there, we visited the farm a number of times and decided to take the leap of moving there the next summer, 1975. I would resign from teaching at Hope College and strike out to this new adventure. It was not an easy decision; even though I was weary of academia, Hope College was a good position and Holland a good city to raise kids. We had a very nice house in a lovely city—near the great Lake Michigan.

This was an enormous adventurous leap for me. Mom often restrained me from exploring some adventuresome experiences that my peers experienced. For instance, some of my friends took what I thought were more exciting summer jobs than I had—following the wheat harvest in the Midwest, which involved driving big trucks and combines; working in the fish industry in Alaska—hard work, but good money, but too far from Pond Bank.

From the lack of taking risks banned by my conservative parents, I think I wanted a more interesting life, to experience as much as I could. I embraced the idea of communal living as a practical solution to pollution, waste, and unnecessary affluence. I thought it was wasteful for everyone to own lawn mowers, laundry appliances, tools, several cars and the like. I thought it would be an opportunity for my wife to start a career, other than teaching, which she had lost interest in. She had worked at an H & R Block office for several years and wanted to pursue something in the bookkeeping, accountant field. I would be the househusband and pursue opportunities as a free-lance musician—to conduct, sing and teach.

I decided to buy a U-Haul type truck to move us across the country and to sell it after we arrived in Washington. I found one in pretty good shape, not too expensive, bought it and sold it in Washington for the exact same price. We bought a pop-out camper to pull behind our Dodge Charger. We had quite the caravan—my wife driving the Charger pulling the camper, me driving the truck and with my great Collie dog, Fritz, lying on the seat beside me. I had a lot of houseplants, my hobby while in Holland, that I didn't want to leave behind. I reserved enough space in the back of the truck bed and made a contraption to hang my plants, with some also on the floor. Every night at the campsite, I would open up the sliding door at the back of the truck to check on them and water them if needed.

Quite a trip! But, we had a good time and arrived at the farm safely after a few twists and turns. One anecdote. We had just left some friends in Nampa, Idaho and were starting the last stretch of our journey, when the truck all of a sudden died. My mechanical abilities are very limited and I used them up in the first several minutes, checking a few things that I knew—the sparkplug wires were all connected; there was water in the radiator, plenty of oil and gas, etc.

A small truck, with a tank on its bed and a gun in a rack behind the seat, pulled up behind us. A scruffy man stepped out and offered to help. I thought that was very generous of him and in a few minutes, he discovered it was an electrical problem that he could fix, but the horn wouldn't work for the rest of the trip—which was OK to me. He even offered to follow us for a while to be certain that the truck didn't stop again. We stopped, at some point, and gave him a grateful thanks and that he could be on his way.

Things, then, got a little creepy—he wondered which route we were taking and claimed it was the same route he was going and that he would camp with us that night. This seemed very suspicious to us and we determined we wouldn't let that happen. We soon came to a junction that gave us a choice of routes—we lied and said that we had an uncle who lived on the other route and we were going to stop to visit him for the night. He, thankfully, said he would go on his way on the other route. I felt bad having such suspicions of him since he helped us so much, but we were a bit frightened, I have to say.

When we arrived at the farm, we realized that families were far behind on their projects and that there was no housing for us. The solution was for us to live in our pop-out camper, for a short while, parked in a little corral near the dilapidated barn. I hung my plants around the camper and on the fence. The horse enjoyed my asparagus fern, eating it down to the soil. We were there for about a month, when our living arrangements went from bad to worse.

Another family, I'll call "Bob and Cindy" moved up from Seattle to join all of us, so now, the community consisted of five families—ten adults and twelve young children. After only a couple of weeks, one of the original couples, " Bill and Sue" who was building a house in the "back forty", decided that it would be more convenient if they lived back there—in our camper. We had a pretty good-sized tent, so they thought we could live in that for a short time.

So, here's the picture. One of the original families was living on the first floor of the old farmhouse, which wasn't in very good shape. The Seattle family of Bob and Cindy with two children, moved into the unfinished, dusty, dirty attic, of that farmhouse, with bad, loose floorboards and no wall covering. Another of the families lived in a partly finished cabin that they were working on, the third one in our camper and us in our tent.

It was one of the most miserable times of my life. Typical Northwest weather, it rained a lot and it became cold and damp in the tent and the ground soggy and muddy. Our clothes, even in a dresser in the tent, were never dry. The stinky outhouse, which was worse than the one on our old home farm, served as our rest room. There was only one bathroom with a tub and shower on the property — in the first floor of the old farmhouse.

The group was working on an old chicken house to make it barely livable for the family now living in first floor of the farmhouse. So by fall the house in the back was finished enough to keep that family warm and dry; the family from the farmhouse moved into the chicken house, with the rats and all. The family living in the small cabin remained there and we moved into the first floor of the farmhouse and the fifth family stayed in the very bare and crude attic.

The original families had worked out some form of governance. I had been attracted to the idea of consensus—like the Quakers. The original three—with mutual respect and trust within a spiritual group—promised that ideal. But when we new couples arrived with our ideas of equality and consensus, it soon became apparent that this created uncertainty in the group. It, also, became clear that Bill and Sue, who had put the most money into the property, had the actual control of the original families.

Part of the goal of establishing a community was to have a self-sustaining lifestyle. None of the first couples had farmed, gardened, animal experience and fumbled trying to learn. They bought an old draft horse they called Gus, asked some neighbors how to hitch him up to a single bottomed plow and tried to turn over the soil for a garden. That was a scene out of a comic reel. Sue was directed to be in charge of planting the garden, even though she grew up in a city and had never gardened before. Now, Bob and I had grown up with gardens, mentored by our fathers, knew so much about proper gardening techniques. Yet we were expected to work in the garden, but not interfere with decisions made. For example, carrot seeds are so small that the tradition is to scatter them in a row, wait until they sprout and then thin out the plants. No, we were instructed to plant these tiny seeds, one by one.

Bill and Sue decided they wanted to have riding horses. So they bought an older Arabian horse, named Sunflower. They knew nothing about horses, but read books on them. I had ridden horses, but can't say I was experienced, but my buddy Bob, the other new man, had grown up with horses. We, however, weren't allowed to ride Sunflower until they had "trained" her. I was so mad at the whole scene by that time, that one morning I saddled up Sunflower and took off riding her rapidly around the corral which probably didn't endear me to some.

It was promised that we newcomers' names would be added to the deed when we arrived and deposited whatever money we could into the property. I had cashed in my TIAA-CREF retirement money of about $4000 to put in the community pot for a share in the property. But we were told soon after arrival that we would not be put on the deed. I was quite upset! Very quickly it was evident that the community was run by a phantom of consensus decision-making. Bill and Sue, when really wanting something against the wishes of the others, would hang on until the rest of us got tired and gave up. We had many very ugly meetings with a lot of confrontation.

To add to the demise of the community, Bill and Sue began evolving into much more radical religious beliefs. They began attending some of the meetings of the cult, the Unification Church, commonly known as the "Moonies" named after their leader, Sun Myong Moon. They never joined, but became more radicalized and emphatic of their special connection to God and Jesus. In one of our meetings, sometime in December of 1975, Sue announced that she had a personal encounter with Jesus, up on the hill, and He said that the two new families had to move off the farm, now. Jesus said we were an evil influence and disrupting the spiritual development of the group.

It was an extremely painful, frustrating and depressing time for me. I said, "Like Hell, I'm going to move, now". I had given up a great job, sold my house in Michigan, moved my family the entire way across the country and now after four months, we had to leave? No way. I told them they would literally have to drag me out of the house. We needed to figure out what our next move would be. We had little money, no place to go, and I was quite depressed.

We had several sources of income. Soon after arriving in the summer, my wife was hired, as a bookkeeper, by a jewelry making company, a rather hippie kind of company that made jewelry out of picture rock jasper. They tried various off beat products, like toe rings, before they became popular and so they didn't sell. Later, a scrimshaw company that etched pictures into fossil ivory, employed her in the same capacity.

I applied to be an adjunct voice teacher at Western Washington University (WWU) in Bellingham. The university had a very good music program and I was pleased to continue to teach, but without involvement in faculty meetings, administrative crap, tenure, etc. I taught about twelve voice students in two days in a beautiful studio that overlooked the Bellingham Bay. I taught a few students at home, as well.

A Presbyterian church in the city needed a music director and conductor of the choir so I applied and was hired. It was not a very talented choir but, again kept my fingers in my profession. Much of our family social life centered on our church friends. These were contrasted with the hippie crowd that my wife worked with. They had wild parties with a lot of booze and pot.

Seeking more professional solo performances, since I wasn't tied down to full time teaching, I sang a number of auditions. I auditioned for Conductor Richard Bonynge, husband of Joan Sutherland, who was the artistic director of the Vancouver Opera Company. I was still only 34 and very scared—the biggest audition of my life. I didn't have much confidence of getting a gig, but what the hell? He was very nice and complimentary, but didn't engage me.

I auditioned for the very respected Merola Young Artists program of San Francisco Opera, but wasn't selected. The feedback was that I had a wonderful musical theater voice—about as bad a critique that a serious singer could get. These and other auditions taught me the very difficult process of becoming a truly profession singer. It was helpful, as later in life I had to advise students.

My faculty status at WWU, gave me the opportunity to perform in as soloist in several oratorios with orchestra; including Bach's *St. John Passion*, Haydn's *Creation* and a number of Haydn and W. A Mozart masses. With the WWU Opera Workshop, I performed Aeneas in Henry Purcell's *Dido and Aeneas* on stage and sang the role of Sarastro in Mozart's *Die Zauberflöte* in a concert version. I loved this role, and it worked with the small orchestra, but my voice was not bass enough and I was too small of stature to have performed it in a full production,

A small theater company in Bellingham engaged me in 1976, to sing the title role in Sousa's opera, *El Capitan*. It was a very small house, so we gave fifteen performances. It's a quite quirky opera, with not very inspired music, but it again put me in costume and on stage.

I performed several recitals WWU and in small tours around the state. The repetition of a program gave me an opportunity to perform a bit differently each night as well as achieve some consistency. One of the biggest concerts was on a community concert series in the Tri-Cities, Washington. A reviewer said, "Lehman produced a beautiful, sonorous, well-supported tone in all registers".

After not studying voice for a couple of years, I wanted to find a respected teacher. I auditioned for Leon Lishner, a well-known opera singer, who was teaching at the University of Washington in Seattle. He opined that I was a bass and attempted to train me in that "fach"—a method of classifying vocal quality and character. It became an interesting experiment, but really wasn't my voice. I did learn more about deepening my sound and connecting it to a lower sense of breathing, which allowed me in future to tackle some of the bass roles in oratorio.

I met several young singers in Bellingham, who moved to Santa Barbara to study with another famous singer, Metropolitan baritone Martial Singher. They liked him and respected him and felt they benefited from his teaching. I traveled to Santa Barbara to study with him for a concentrated two weeks. In addition to teaching me, he allowed me to sit in on a number of his other lessons. Not only did the lessons improve my singing but, both of these teachers gave me new ideas, some that I put in my "bag of tricks of teaching" for future reference.

In the spring of 1976, we rented a very small, but nice house in Bellingham. To the kids' memories, it will always be the little red house. But, I felt we needed investment in a property. The next summer, 1977, I found the perfect house—a fixer upper. It needed a lot of cosmetic work, which I knew I could accomplish, since I wasn't working full time and I had experience in carpentry.

A single mother, who lost her husband in the Vietnam War, was depressed and let the house deteriorate in many ways. She bought a house trailer and wanted to sell her house, "as is", and not look back. The kitchen sinks were filled with dirty dishes, pots and pans; there were puncture holes in one bedroom wall, where her early teen son put his fist. There were broken toys in a pile and a Franklin stove in the middle of the living room on a beautiful oak flooring that needed refinishing. The second floor bathroom was framed in but not finished, a closet was in disarray and the outside shingles badly needed paint.

We bought it for a very reasonable price, and I began immediately to work on it. A good friend loaned us a small camping trailer that we parked in the driveway while we rolled up our sleeves and tackled all the projects. The kitchen had to be cleaned and disinfected. I took many pick-up truckloads of stuff to the dump. In the next year, I refinished the hardwood floors in the dining room and living room, finished the upstairs bathroom, fixed the closet, painted the exterior, and much more. It was a good foray back into building things with my hands.

I enjoyed being a househusband as well. I liked the ability to decide my schedule and the freedom from a system of administration. I have always enjoyed cooking, and since I wasn't working full time I began to cook most of our meals. Cooking became a hobby that I enjoy to this day. Later, when I was single and would come home from teaching, dead tired, I found it refreshing to cook a nice meal, just for me.

The ability to spend more time with my kids was an added treat. When Gina was pre-school we had a lot of fun together with a lot of activities. One of our favorites was to drive down to the Bellingham pier to the fish market and get fresh Dungeness crab for lunch. I trucked the kids to their music lessons. Scott was studying Suzuki violin that requires a parent to attend the lessons in order to aid in the students practice at home.

As long as I can remember, I have had an attachment to water. I don't know why—our family didn't live near water, we couldn't go to any public beaches because of the flesh showing swimsuits, so I didn't learn to swim until I was 25. I loved going with my Dad and brothers deep sea fishing, just sitting on the beach watching the waves and observing the gulls. I drooled over the boats, of all sizes in the Holland marina.

When looking out my studio at WWU, I watched the boats sail and motor around. I enjoyed the beautiful ferry rides through the San Juan Islands, hoping to see whales. The San Juan Islands number over a hundred that have names. The islands are fascinating places with quaint villages, artistic communities and fishing towns. An optometrist from my church choir owned a very nice cabin cruiser and invited our family, on a number of Sunday afternoons, for trips to the smaller islands.

I dreamed many times of cruising the San Juan's in my own boat. After finally receiving my investment money back from the farm people, I bought a used, older 21 ft. boat to fulfill that dream. It really didn't have a closed cabin, but a solid top covered the cockpit. A canvas tarp—bimini in boating terms—could be unfurled to cover the rest of the boat at nights or in bad weather. A table, with two bench seats, folded down into a bed for two and there were two small berths in the bow for the kids. The little propane cook stove allowed us to cook simple meals and when we docked at marinas we connected to their electricity.

We motored out for a weekend with the kids and enjoyed sleeping on the water. We traveled some distances to visit the larger islands of Orcas, Friday Harbor, San Juan and some small ones, like Doe Island. If the island lacked a dock, I anchored a short distance off shore and row to land in the small dingy on the boat or sometimes I swam ashore, not always with a bathing suit.

My flexible schedule allowed me time to take trips alone, to enjoy the peace and quiet of the water, and work on my emotional shit. One of my favorite journeys was about a half hour ride to an unnamed island only an acre, but had a nice dock.

One day, a friend, who had an exchange student from France, asked if we would host her for a week. I took her for a trip on the boat and in the middle of our journey, we were surprised to see a pod of about a dozen orca whales swimming by. I cut the engine and we sat there, within 15 yards of them—watched them jump, play, do flips just like in a sea park, but this was their natural habitat. What a thrill! The French girl exclaimed "big fish". I tried to explain to her that they were not big fish, but mammals. It didn't work with her broken English and my almost none existing French, until we arrived home and I got out my French/English dictionary.

As the years sped by, I realized that Bellingham was not the place from which to do a lot of professional singing. Even though I was successful in singing in small venues with local groups, one really had to be in the big cities of Seattle and/or Vancouver to truly try his wings. Although I was enjoying being a househusband and father, enjoying the flexibility of my schedule while supporting my itch for music by teaching part time and performing, I knew it was not good to have big a gap in my full time teaching resume should I want to return to academia.

I was told when I began teaching at WWU that there might be an opening for a full time position, but I could see that it was not going to happen. Thus, I began searching for teaching positions all over the US. I applied to some geographic locations where I really didn't want to live, like the South, the hot, boring states of Nebraska, Ohio, etc., but I needed a job. I interviewed and auditioned at a few schools but was not hired.

During the summer of 1978 I applied to, what I thought would be wonderful positions in beautiful New England, Keene State College (KSC) in Keene, NH and University of Maine in Bangor. I was a finalist at both places, but not interviewed nor hired. Late in August, I got a call from Keene saying that they wanted to fly me in for an interview, as their first hire backed out of his contract to take the position at the University of Maine.

As I flew over the Monadnock region—the region named after the highest mountain in southern New Hampshire, Mount Monadnock--from Boston Logan Airport to Keene in a relatively small plane, I was awed by the view of the mountains, lakes, forests and farms. The interview went very smoothly with the Dean of Arts and Humanities and a few of the music faculty.

Since it was primarily a choral position, I was not required to perform. However, a couple of the fine singers--performance majors—requested that I teach a sample lesson. I was shown around town, a lovely small town of about 25,000 residents. It looked like a wonderful place to settle in for a while and raise a family. Another attraction was the plethora of cultural events in the area, in which Keene was about the center

So, late in the summer, I was hired by Keene State College to begin teaching that fall. and I began my career there that lasted 35 years. My wife and the kids stayed in Washington to sell the house, to wrap up her job, and to—with sadness for me—sell the boat. We sold the house, and as hoped, for a good profit that allowed us to buy a house in Keene, into which we moved in January of 1979

Our trip East in a small 1976 Subaru station wagon with Fritz, my big collie, and two kids was an epic journey. We took the Northern, most direct routes, across the country. It, of course, was the dead of winter everyplace. We stopped at a motel in Coeur d'Alene, Idaho with the temperature in the minus 30s and a wind chill that carried it to 50 degrees below 0. The kids remember that it was so cold that at the motel Fritz wouldn't go outside to pee, but held it all night. The car's gas line froze so it had to be towed into a heated garage to sit all night. I found out quickly that products like Ice Out and other additives were necessities in a cold climate.

"Wall Drug" is a joke among travelers through the upper Midwest. There are huge billboards, a hundred or more miles away, advertising exotic animals, real Indian chiefs, animated battles, unique gifts, etc. We got sucked in on one of our trips through there and it is the biggest tourist trap in the country. Their exotic animals consist of a scrawny brown bear, a couple of snakes, a skunk, their Indian chief—a carved chief at the entrance--and shabby cheap gifts.

We had some car trouble near the interstate exit to Wall Drug. Since it was Sunday afternoon and no mechanic garage was open, we had no option but to find a motel and wait until Monday morning. We made friends, at the motel, with a nice young couple that was moving west with a U-Haul truck. We played cards, talked of our lives and our new adventures. They accompanied me to the car shop and brought us back to the motel to play more games and entertain our kids.

I inquired of the woman at the motel desk, the owner's wife, if we could stay past the check out time, without being charged an extra night, if our car was not fixed in time. She assured us that, under the circumstances, it would be fine. About 2:00 p.m., we got our car back and I went to check out and pay our bill. The owner informed me that we would have to pay for two nights since we stayed beyond check out time. I informed him that his wife, who now was not around, told us it was OK and we wouldn't be charged. He insisted and I resisted probably a little too angrily. He called the sheriff, who arrived in his squad car and promptly, said: "You will pay your bill or you will see the inside of a jail cell tonight". I never felt so boxed in with no options in my life. I wondered if that is what African Americans felt like many times.

So, after paying two nights on our credit card, we were on our way. We had car trouble again in upper New York. This time a kind stranger drove me to a nearby gas station for the battery, or whatever it was that we needed. The kids and my wife huddled with the big hairy Fritz to keep warm. As I said, the trip was epic and one my children still love to talk about.

Keene, New Hampshire 1978

WE MOVED INTO OUR BIG old colonial house in a suburb of Keene with a big backyard and many wonderful old features. However, one old feature—lack of insulation—was a problem. Coming from the Northwest where 15 degrees above zero was cold, we thought we would freeze in that old drafty house when it was 26 below zero the first week after we arrived. Our fuel bill was sky high and we knew we had to do something. So, the next summer we had the insulation blown in and purchased a very good Vermont Castings wood burning stove.

That summer, I was so proud of my budding New England traditions by buying and splitting, by hand, nine cords of wood, stacking it all around the backyard. I tilled up a fairly large portion of lawn for a garden—about 20 by 50 feet. I used all my skills learned on the farm to create a huge garden that, as I learned from my parents, greatly supplemented our budget. I hired a contractor to build a greenhouse that attached to the kitchen where I started many of my plants from seeds. One year, I started many melon plants that yielded over 50 melons—watermelons, cantaloupes, cranshaws and honey-dews. I structured tepee-like stands from branches on which I grew beautiful pole beans. The total effect was a cacophony of colors and smells. One of my shrinks told me that I was a gardener to please Daddy and academician to please Mom. I am after all a Gemini.

It was with some eager anticipation that I moved back into an academic atmosphere, even with its politics, to start anew, feeling much more comfortable and competent than starting my first position at Hope College.

Keene State was quite a traditional college with northeast values. I was a little surprised they hired me, since I still dressed like a hippy—flowered shirts, floppy pants and shoulder length hair. I showed some old pictures to students just a few years ago and they hooted with laughter. I am sure it was the Dean of Arts and Humanities, who didn't dress like me, but still had the hippy attitude, and I'm sure influenced my employment.

I was hired to be the director of the choral/vocal department. I conducted the Concert Choir and the Chamber singers. I taught private voice, choral methods, started an Opera Workshop, taught a Music Appreciation class, and over the years taught every thing vocal, mostly courses I developed—Vocal literature, Diction for Singers, and Vocal Pedagogy.

The music faculty consisted of five full time tenure track members before I came and about 80 student majors. I had developed a sense of high standards from graduate school, from the very excellent liberal arts school of Hope College and from teaching at a fine institution like Western Washington University. The idealism that I espoused sometimes put me in conflict with the more traditional faculty. As I like to say, "in those days I was a bit—or maybe more than a bit—full of piss and vinegar".

I am a quite passionate person in a lot of ways and I was passionate about raising the standards of performances and of music education. I wanted the students to have the kind of education, even in a small department in a small college, that they might receive at a better, more well known institution.

Being an active performer, I was particularly concerned about the degree called "Applied Music" which we would call today, a Performance degree. The auditions to get into the program lacked integrity with very little checkpoints or hurdles for the student to pass as they went from year to year. There were no end-of-the-semester juries—performances in front of faculty members to judge their progress—a must at most music schools. I instituted juries for all those taking voice lessons. Music education majors had to give a short senior recital and the applied music majors a short junior recital and a full senior recital. Unlike most schools, there were no qualifying juries to be sung in front of faculty to determine if the student was well enough prepared to sing a public recital.

This problem raised its gory head in my first year. A voice student of mine, an" Applied Music" major, was not prepared to give her senior recital at the level that was respectable for that degree. I told this young lady that I wouldn't allow her to give her recital. My experience in the good vocal programs the voice teacher always made the final decision whether the student could give the recital, even with qualifying juries.

I was surprised to receive a call from the Dean's office to discuss the problem. I gave a litany of the standards that she didn't meet. He wondered if it really was important to me that she not present her recital. I replied that it was very important to establish the standards that I expected for my integrity and the reputation of the college. He informed me that the student confided in another music faculty member that she was going to accuse me of inappropriate behavior in the studio. It never happened, but I wasn't prepared to go through the rigor of a defense. The student gave her poor recital and graduated. After that, I pushed hard for qualifying pre-recital juries—which they had to pass by a vote of a panel of faculty members before being allowed to precede with their public recital. The music faculty finally instituted it.

I sought to develop the KSC music program to the quality of standards held at music schools across the country. I thought my best students should be able to compete respectfully at contests held by such organizations as National Association of Teachers of Singing, (NATS). I felt that when they auditioned for fine graduate schools, they should be accepted at a number of them. I held to those standards all my years and was fortunate enough to have winners at NATS contests, state, regional and nationally and have students graduate from some of the best music schools and conservatories in the country.

Personally, the bad experience at the farm, the betrayal of close friends, left me with a lot of wounds. Even though I now had a great job, enjoyed Keene, created a huge, successful garden in our back yard, was regularly performing and had made good friends, I was not sleeping well and had this cloud of sadness over me. My sister and I coined the phrase "We don't do happy very well" –learned from my mother—so I let it slide.

However, it persisted and I decided I needed some counseling to get a professional, doctor's perspective. My family doctor recommended a well-known local psychiatrist. He heard my story and diagnosed evidence of a chemical depression—common in my Lehman family, we came to realize over the years.

He started me on an antidepressant. In 1980, the medications were not as specific as they are now and we had to experiment with a number them to find one that was compatible with my singing and teaching. Many of them gave me dry mouth, which was horrible for my voice.

My counselor turned from the farm events to other issues of my past, including my upbringing in the Mennonite way of life, my parents, the guilt of the evangelical beliefs, my feminine side, my musical goals and much more. He told me that the farm was only the catalyst that drew out the symptom of the illness. The medication alleviated most of those symptoms and allowed me to live a more even keel life.

Our children were now ages six and eight and our thoughts turned to how we wanted to teach them about spiritual things. My parents were very concerned about their religious education. By this time, I was well aware of the damage inflicted on my emotions, morality and spirituality, by the guilt laden childhood experiences in Sunday school and church. I didn't want to subject my children to those experiences.

We attended a number of churches in Keene, but weren't satisfied with any of them. We began a search for the closest Mennonite church. It was in Vermont, about an hour's drive. We attended it once and found it to be too close to our upbringing of evangelical dogma. We heard about a Mennonite Church in Boston that met on Sunday evenings in members' homes. We visited it one Sunday and, although, it was a very inconvenient distance, about one and a half hours, we opted to attend about every other week and become members.

The congregation was made up of an eclectic group of people who came from similar backgrounds as ours. Many were involved in academe—professors at Harvard, Boston University, Northeastern, University of New Hampshire, Mennonite graduate and undergraduate students in Boston to attend school, as well as business people, medical personnel, etc. A church council governed the congregation; including selecting a rotating lay minister.

The services were very informal with wonderful four part congregational singing, discussions of current issues, sometimes a homily. Many of the members came from Mennonite colleges with choral experience. Some evenings we rehearsed parts of a major choral work that some members had sung previously and sang them in an informal performance, just for ourselves. Sometimes there were instrumentalists who would accompany, but usually just with piano. We performed parts of the *Messiah*, Fauré's *Reguiem*, Mozart and Haydn masses, which I was usually asked to conduct.

It was a very invigorating collection of people with discussions that continued to evolve my spiritual life and move me along on my spiritual journey.

A highlight was the yearly retreat, an over night, in some lovely spot, such as Cape Cod, or in a camp in Breton Woods. These 24 hours together allowed us to explore more deeply some topics and to interact more informally with each other. I will always remember one of these informal conversations with Gordon Kauffman at one of the retreats.

Gordon was a highly respected professor of theology at Harvard for many years, had written a number of books on the concept of God. The verbiage used to express his ideas in his books was often too deep for this "lay" person, but in a conversation he spoke at a more practical, understandable level. In one of those Cape conversations, we were discussing God and how the belief of an omnipotent God has caused some horrible, historical events to occur in His name. There were Christian wars, persecution of those of a different faith, Christians hurting other Christians—such as the persecution of our forefathers, the Anabaptists—Muslims killing other Muslims, all the while, chanting God is great, all because they assumed their connection to God was the only correct way. Gordon expressed that his God was a God of "questions", not of "answers". If one believes his/her view of God is the only correct way and feels that God's instructions were to perform these deeds—no matter how they run counter to the morals of the world—he/she feels empowered to act.

Gordon's affirmation of my growing, changing attitude toward God, learned from the church experiences of my childhood, was a life long gift to me as I struggled to find my spiritual core that I knew was there, but was not massaged by going to church.

I read a number of books by such current "gurus" as Gerald G. Jampolski's *Love is Letting go of Fear*, Scott Peck's *The Road Less Traveled* and the *People of the Lie*, Henri J. M. Nouwen's *Be here now,* and others. I attended a few seminars by some of these authors on meditation, living in the present, etc. I kept coming back to finding God in the small things, in nature, in great music, in other people. I've probably had more spiritual experiences in music, whether performing or listening, than in anything else.

The Boston Congregation didn't have a Sunday school per se. They tried, in every service, to have some story or activity for the children. I did want my children to know some of the old classic stories from the Bible, to be educated in them. A lot of Bible storybooks recited moral conclusions from the story, often messages of the old fundamental tenets. We searched and found an old version of a Bible storybook that simply told the story and didn't project a moral bias or judgment on them, particularly those of the Old Testament. We read these to our kids, often at bedtime, as we did other books. We taught them about morality, peace and justice issues, about responsibility to one's neighbor as we saw it.

Another huge event occurred in the early 80's—Daddy was diagnosed with prostate cancer—Mom called it "prostrate" cancer. He received all of the normal procedures used to slow or neutralize the cancer, but none of them really worked. This was a testing time for my faith. Daddy was the epitome of the devout, of the faithful. He was not perfect, but his faith was deep within him.

It was difficult for me to be living so distant from him. And at the beginning, my parents had conflicting memories of the doctor's conversations at the office visits. My siblings tried to translate for me, but it was very frustrating for me. I found out the name of his oncologist, found his phone number and gave his office a call. I announced to the nurse that this was Dr. Carroll Lehman, son of Andrew Lehman who was a patient of So-and-So, and I would like to speak to him about my father's condition. The doctor called me back and launched into very technical aspects of Dad's diagnosis and his treatment. I asked some dumb questions and the MD, said; "They told me that you are a Doctor?" I had to fess up that I was, but not a medical doctor. Luckily, he thought it was kind of funny and explained Daddy's condition in more "Lehman's" terms.

I visited Daddy every other weekend if I could. I caught the train in Brattleboro, Vermont about midnight, arrived in Lancaster about 8:00 a.m., borrowed a car from my sister and drove to Chambersburg to be at his bedside most of the weekend, whether at home or the hospital. I jumped on the train in Lancaster midmorning on Sunday, arrived back in Brattleboro about 1:00 a.m. Monday and went to work.

As devout a person as Dad was, I believe this tested his faith as well—he was only 69 when diagnosed and 71 when he died. It was amazing to me to hear what some—I think well intentioned—people said to him. He was told a number of times that this was God's will, even if he didn't understand it and such thing as "God's ways are not our ways", "he who the Lord loves He chastened". He was told that he was not being healed because he lacked faith. I would get so pissed when I witnessed some of these conversations.

I read the book by Rabbi Harold S. Kushner, *When Bad Things Happen to good People,* trying to get some perspective of reason. It was a great affirmation of my belief that God after the setting spin of the creation had to permit it to function on its own. Otherwise, how would He decide that a faithful man like Dad got ill and died and an evil person lived a long life? How did He decide to honor the prayers of the farmer who wanted rain for his crops, or the farmer next door who prayed for his hay not to get wet? A statement in Kushner's book that seemed to sum up his view—and meant a lot to me—was that "God was crying too".

As the cancer progressed, Daddy went in and out of clear consciousness. During one of my visits, Daddy was just coming out of one of his "hallucination" periods when he sensed that I was sitting by his bedside with Mom. He mystically looked at me, and exclaimed, "Carroll, did you ride the motorcycle here?" Mom tried to chide him, "No, Andrew, you are hallucinating." Daddy persisted, "Did you ride the motorcycle here, Carroll? If you did, I can ride it home for you." Now, my Dad had never ridden a motorcycle, to my knowledge, and certainly it wouldn't have been appropriate behavior, particularly in my mom's eyes—he being an officer in the Mennonite church, a mature man—and would have been too dangerous with too much of a risk for her.

I was fascinated by this outburst, so uncharacteristic of my daddy. But, the more I pondered it and discussed it with my sister, the more it became a theme for the rest of my life. To this day, I believe that it was a metaphor for life—a life that Daddy didn't have and couldn't have had, in his Mennonite context, in his marriage, but maybe one he dreamed of. I believe there were numerous times that he dreamed of having a more adventuresome life than the one that always needed to be of common sense, a life that was kind of thrust upon him.

At times, we could get him to tell stories of his childhood and early adult life. We reveled in some of the pranks and "naughty" deeds he imposed on his brothers or friends. Sometimes he would laugh, as he told them, until tears ran down his cheek, to our great delight.

Being less adventurous and not really having the money to take big trips, my parent's first plane trip was to Iowa after Scott was born. They drove to Michigan a couple times while we were there and they flew out to Washington to visit us on the farm. We rented a RV and had a wonderful trip down the coast of Washington and Oregon.

I chose to ride the "motorcycle"—"the road less traveled"—more than did my parents or my siblings. Those decisions, like the farm, didn't always have the desired outcome, but enriched my life.

We knew the end was approaching when Daddy went into a coma one Friday night and we all rushed to his side. The doctor told us that he, probably, wouldn't make it through the weekend. But, he woke up on Monday morning and lived another horrible month.

When I visited him a couple weeks later, before his death, J. Mark Stauffer—my old music professor—who was the chaplain at my parents' retirement home, came into the room. In the conversation, Daddy looked up at

Mark, with painful eyes, and asked; "Why, Mark, why". For once a minister, a devout person said back to Daddy the truth; "Andy, I don't know. I would like to say some platitude, but I don't know."

I'm standing in the corner in a puddle of tears and as Mark left, he laid his hand on my shoulder and said; "I'm very sorry, Carroll, I wish I had some answer for him and you, but I don't"—finally, a man of God giving a sensible and believable answer. He never knew how much that meant to me. Memories flooded back of my discussion with Gordon Kauffman—my God is a God of questions not answers.

Daddy died on Father's Day weekend in 1983. His life was far too short, but when I once asked him about that, he said he had a good life and that he experienced far more than he ever thought he would.

One night after he passed away and before his memorial service an incredible thing happened. I woke up in the middle of the night at my parent's home and heard a whip-poor-will, a bird with a wonderful unique call, that was very special to our family. They are a nocturnal bird and when I was a kid, sometimes just after dark, one would sit in our old crab apple tree, a short distance from our house and sing and sing. Many times we boys, even if we were already in bed, would crawl out and put on our pants, get a spotlight and try to see him. I hadn't heard his call for years and years. I know it was sent to somewhat palliate my grief.

Meanwhile my life went on. After trying to establish some kind of a career as soloist in Washington, I was determined to continue to pursue as many performing opportunities as possible, even while teaching full time. I enjoyed performing and it was fulfilling musically, personally and spiritually.

In the fall of 1978, soon after I arrived in Keene, I saw a notice for an audition for soloists for the Haydn *Creation* with the New Hampshire Symphony. I made an appointment to sing for the conductor and he hired me, on the spot, to sing the part of Adam who appears in the second half with a number of beautiful duets with Eve.

The next big break came when I was engaged to sing with a new opera company, Opera North, based in Lebanon, NH. They were performing the *The Marriage of Figaro* by Mozart and I auditioned for any of the appropriate roles. One might recall that I sang the role of Figaro in graduate school. This time, however, the director chose me to sing the role of Dr. Bartolo, a comic, buffo role. It was a lot of fun, and I seemed to get the best reviews from comic roles.

These performances gave me, in the area, some legitimacy as a professional, capable soloist. In the eighties and nineties, I sang, again, with the New Hampshire Symphony, a couple of times with the Nashua Symphony, and many of the choral ensembles—including Plymouth, Concord, Keene, Monadnock—in performances of some of the great choral works with orchestra.

For a short time I sang with a small group called Through the Opera Glass that performed scenes from operas in schools, for banquets, fundraisers, etc. One summer we toured with the Vermont Symphony around many venues in Vermont, including in the meadow of the Trapp family estate.

A small company, on the seacoast of New Hampshire named V-O-C-A-L called me out of the blue one day in 1986 and asked if I would sing the role of Guglielmo in Mozart's *Cosi van tutte*. The baritone that they had hired made a trip to the dentist and a procedure went bad and broke his jaw. The performance was only a month away so I had to learn quickly. Fortunately, the school year had just ended so I could fully concentrate on the role. They liked me and invited me to play the Count, in Mozart's *The Marriage of Figaro*, my third different bass baritone role in that opera.

Throughout those early years at Keene State, I sang several full-length faculty recitals and performed them in several venues around the state. The New England venues were not Carnegie Hall, but I was pleased to be performing many of the great compositions, ones that I loved.

Cancun 1982 −2012

In 1982, my wife and I decided to escape from the harsh winter for a week in Cancun, Mexico. We bought one of those deals often advertised in travel magazines and papers. We chose a week beginning on January 6 at the Flamingo hotel, located amidst the hotel district on the spit that runs south out of the town of Cancun. It was refreshing, to say, the least, to lie on the beach, look at the ocean and feel warm.

One day, as we lay on the beach, a person came by advertising a new resort nearby and offered a free breakfast if we stopped by to see it. Of course, they then tried to sell us a timeshare. We had noticed, from the beach, this unique building among the much bigger unattractive hotels. Being owned by a wealthy Mexican, Club Baccara was painted in bright, various colors—the structure had interesting facades with many different shapes of windows.

We bought the timeshare for a fixed week, the first week in January for 25 years. Baccara offered for me many memorable experiences over those years with some interesting twists and turns.

Soon after we bought the timeshare, one of the worst hurricanes ever known to Cancun came through and effected much destruction among the hotel strip. Baccara was severely damaged and I thought we had, probably, lost our investment.

The January after the hurricane, we still went to Cancun, but stayed in a cheap motel. We went to Baccara to watch the restoration effort. The big resorts, owned mostly by Americans, absorbed all the heavy equipment so we watched as Mayan laborers, literally, broke up the concrete with sledge hammers, put the pieces in plastic five gallon buckets, and carried them out to the street. A rickety, loosely assembled, wooden staircase descended to the beach.

But it did come back. While we were there we took the opportunity to learn more about Mexico. In the early 80's, Cancun and the area around it was still very crude and poor. The buses belched smoke from its exhaust, shaking and rattling down the road. They were often packed with workers with unpleasant odors. The taxis cost what you were able to negotiate with the driver in dilapidated cars, who sped through the streets like mad men.

That part of Mexico is dotted with a number of amazing Mayan ruins, reminiscent of the Greek ruins. The Mayans had built a very sophisticated culture and civilization, for that time—around 1000 AD. Their ruins demonstrate their sophisticated knowledge of mathematics, astronomy, and calendric. One year we rented a little VW bug which was falling apart and drove south to visit the Tulum ruins site. The larger, more spectacular Chechen Itza was the first of four Seven Wonders of the World on several lists—there are different lists—that I have had the privilege of visiting over the years, the others were the Great Wall of China, the Rome coliseum, and leaning tower of Pisa.

In the past few years with my wife Marcia, we made very good friends of several couples, who came to Baccara each year on the same week as we did. Blake, a retired defense lawyer from Chattanooga, Tennessee became as close to me as a brother. He and I are both very liberal in politics and religion. We spent hours by the pool deeply discussing the meaning of both and of life itself.

Our experiences included this scary story with a good ending. In 2011, Marcia and I were at the airport, about an hour from our flight home, when Marcia began feeling sick and decided to walk it off. When she came back, she was in such pain. I have never seen anyone in that level of agony—she was crying, writhing on the floor and threw up. A nice man nearby came over, said he was a trained EMT and asked if he could help. He almost immediately said Marcia needed a Doctor, so he went to the ticket counter and asked for a doctor. It seemed forever, but a doctor did arrive who was very nice and knowledgeable. She took us to a small infirmary in the airport and after an examination said she thought Marcia was suffering from pancreatitis or gastritis and should be taken by ambulance, immediately to a hospital. You can image the fearful pictures that flew through my brain—a Mexican ambulance, a Mexican hospital? But the ambulance was in excellent condition, fairly well equipped and the crew was truly professional and helpful.

Marcia was taken to a private hospital, newly built of about three years before—about the cleanest hospital I have ever seen—still very worried, but more relaxed. They had all modern equipment of sonograms, x-rays, MRI machines, etc. They soon determined that Marcia had pancreatitis and needed to stay in the hospital.

The manager at Baccara, who had become a very good friend, was simply wonderful and amazing. Humberto gave me a room to stay in until we could leave for home. He went to the airport and somehow persuaded the officers to give him our luggage, visited Marcia in the hospital numerous times.

Now, we had to make payment to the hospital before Marcia could be released. I tried to think of the credit cards we had along and how much we had available. Marcia spent several hours in the ER, had many tests, remained in the hospital for three days, was given numerous drugs and was treated by a wonderful specialist. When I looked at the bill, given to me as we were about to leave, I only saw the numbers 32......., I immediately thought $32,000, and figured that wasn't too bad. When I got to the cashier, she says no, it is $3200.

We do have a problem here in the states with medical treatment. In comparison, I just recently had an ablation procedure—one that freezes a small part of the heart that is causing atrial fibrillation, which I have had for years. It is a very tricky procedure, performed by a highly skilled doctor, I was in the operating room for about six hours, stayed only one night in the hospital, but my bill was over $100,000, yes, one hundred thousand dollars.

My contract for Baccara is now up, but it's OK, because the ownership of Baccara, now named something else, changed once again, and the last time we were there the old staff was gone, our Tennessee friends had some health problems and didn't come. But, I have great memories of Cancun and events that added much to my life experiences.

Europe 1984

ONE OF THE GREATEST PERKS of teaching at a college/university is the sabbatical. Every six years you can apply for a sabbatical—a semester off with full pay or a full year with half pay. You write a proposal of your study, writing, and travel and how it relates to your teaching goals and aspirations, to be evaluated by an elected committee of faculty peers for approval. I proposed a sabbatical for the fall of 1984 to accomplish my desire to live and study in Europe for a semester.

High on my bucket list, even at the age of 42, was to live in Europe—soak up the culture, visit musically historical places, hear concerts in great venues, learn German better, and study voice with a new teacher. I asked my old professor from Iowa, Mr. Gammon, if he had any recommendations. He said that a baritone, Rudolf Knoll, had just given a successful master class at Iowa, and he opined that he could be helpful to me.

I had never ventured so distant, for this length of time, alone. I was thrilled and a bit frightened simultaneously. I yearned to travel like this, as a youth, but it was far out of my parent's comfort zone. This was almost exactly one year after Daddy died and the first time I felt I was following his metaphoric admonition to ride the motorcycle. On my journeys in Europe, any church, cathedral, large or small, that had candles to light, I lit one for him, with a moment of silence.

I flew to Frankfurt in May, rented a car at the airport to travel North to visit a couple of exchange students, who had studied at KSC, one of which lived with us. I remember loitering in the airport before my huge leap out into the unknown. I finally headed out on to the Autobahn—freeway--in my small, cheap car with little power. The Audis, Mercedes and Volvos were flying by me at 90+ miles per hour. I pulled over several times to take a deep breath.

In a small town, near Bremen, I found our exchange student, Uva's house. I was dead tired, but had to be sociable with his family, who spoke no English. I had promised Uva that I would attempt to only speak German when I visited him, as he spoke English when he lived with us. I struggled but managed, with some help from him.

From Bremen I traveled farther North for a trip around Denmark, just to get a taste of Scandinavia. My first stop was in Copenhagen, an amazing city, with its Tivoli Gardens, the harbor, the oldest buildings that I had ever seen, and physically beautiful people. I stayed the first night in a Youth Hostel, trying to save money. I bunked in a large room with about 20 young men, most who stayed out late and came in drunk about 2 o'clock—loud, noisy and obnoxious.

I looked in my travel book and found a really cheap, downtown hotel. I moved there in the afternoon and didn't realize until the lights came on at night that I was smack in the middle of the "Red Light" district. I went to a bar for drinks, the TV was on behind the bar, I looked and to my amazement it was not sports being broadcast, but the vilest porn one can imagine.

I had a great time. I saw that the great mezzo-soprano, Krista Ludwig, a person that I had listened to on recordings many, many times, was giving a recital in the concert hall of Tivoli, so I jumped at the chance to hear her in person. Afterward I enjoyed the sights and atmosphere of Tivoli, including a Ferris wheel ride, sitting across from a lovely young mother and her small son. We got stuck at the top of the wheel for a number of minutes and we talked each other out of fright.

My travel book told me that you don't go down to the wharf at night for it was a choice spot for sailors who could become drunken, rowdy and dangerous, but I wanted to experience it. So while there was still light, I edged into a bar with a nice looking man and woman, sat at the bar beside a Finnish man who had a fair amount to drink, but we had a fascinating conversation about

Scandinavians—the tensions between the Finns and the rest, etc. I scooted out of the bar with a group of people and hurried back to the hotel.

The next few days, I skirted around the edge of Denmark with a number of stops and headed south to Salzburg, my home until December.

The division of the East and West became clear as I looked on the map and saw that all the roads leading to the East stopped at the border. I wanted to go to Berlin, to Leipzig—some of the cities associated with music history, but I was fearful. There was "checkpoint Charlie" but I didn't feel safe crossing it alone.

I stopped for an overnight in Lubeck and, after checking into the hotel, visited the Mariankircke—a church where J.S. Bach spent some time. I rode up the elevator to one of the steeples with a nice young lady and I started to speak German to her, but she quickly switched to English. She was from Norway and staying in Lubeck serving her internship to become a medical doctor. She found out I was a musician and was very curious and inquisitive. I invited her to a café to continue our discussion. She asked me a question that I pondered many times over the years. "Does one have to be a Christian to perform well a work like the St. Matthew's Passion and portray Jesus, or a prophet? I thought a while and said that a devout person might perform it more from the soul, but a good acting singer could also perform it sincerely. I said that I had played roles in opera that I hoped I didn't need to replicate in real life to be authentic.

As I continued the next day down through Germany, it was a very hot day with no air conditioning in the car. I decided to find a lake and go for a swim. I found one on the map, parked the car, changed to my swimming suit and followed people to the beach. I quickly learned that Europeans are much more comfortable with their bodies than we are. As I looked around, I realized that I was the only man with a boxer-type swimming suit—all the Germans were wearing speedos.

While enjoying the sun a group of, I would guess, college age youths came running through the beach and into the water—boys with speedos, girls topless. All the people on the beach, men and women, were obviously enjoying the scenery. When I stopped in München to visit the famous English

Gardens, many people were sitting around on blankets in various stages of undress. You could encounter a nude person on one of the paths or sitting eating their picnic lunch. I tried to look cool, but probably didn't.

I had enrolled in the summer academy of the Mozarteum, a very famous conservatory, where Herr Knoll led a four-week master class in vocal performance. We met 2-4 hours each day. There were about 20 students, some of them observers. We participants were required to be prepared to sing every day. Knoll gave us pointers and instructions on vocal technique and vocal style—both art song and opera—that would improve our singing. I learned, not only from his instructions to me, but by observing his coaching of the other singers.

He was a very good teacher, but a mean SOB. He was very blunt and direct in his instructions, but you couldn't allow him to get under your skin. One student from the states thought he was being criticized too harshly and began to retort, in tears, to Knoll. He might as well have gone home after that, for Knoll wouldn't give him the time of day. I was, by some years, the oldest in the class, but I was not immune from his rants. One day after I had sung, he grabbed me by the arm, shoved me in front of the mirror and said: "Why don't you do—such and such—I told you yesterday how to do it".

The students came from around the world to this class—many from the states, some from South Africa, Germany, Japan and Korea. English was the functional language for this diverse group of singers. I made many friends, some who stayed after the summer to study privately with Herr Knoll as I did. He taught after the summer class at his beautiful home in the "Sound of Music" land. A friend and I would schedule consecutive lessons and when we alit from the bus, we had about a half-mile hike to his house. As typical of Europe, several benches lined the path, where you could sit and admire the marvelous hills and valleys of the Alpine foothills. Herr Knoll often invited us to stay for beers and bratwurst and to just shoot the breeze. He loved to tell stories, particularly of his singing at the Met, on his fellow singers and conductors, of singing in Vienna, etc.

I impressed him enough with my voice that he agreed to arrange auditions with a couple of agents. In Europe, you sing for an agent and if he likes you, he will arrange an audition for a particular opera house. I knew of this system from friends, but wanted to experience myself.

He set me up with auditions for two agents, with very different results. I sang for one of the most famous in München—I was the last singer of the day. It was in a very small room, the agent wasn't listening and talked with his assistant most of the time. The second was in Essen where the agent listened carefully to my performance, asked for a second and third aria. At the conclusion, he looked in his book for some small houses where he would send me. But, I had to come back to my job and my family.

Almost every weekend, I took advantage of traveling by train to small towns and large cities. Trains are so convenient in Europe, something I miss in the States. It seems so silly that we have torn up many of the tracks for trails for snowmobiles, while many other countries are improving their systems with high-speed trains and better service. One of the handy aspects of traveling by train was the convenience of a travel office located in many of the train stations that offered services to aid in finding housing for your stay. We told the agents that we were on foot, how much we wanted to pay, what desired location, and they would made the phone reservation, instruct us in public transportation and we were set.

Sometimes when I would be alone and traveling through small towns, I stayed an overnight at a "Zimmer frei"—room free—if it was near the station. These were, what we would call, Bed & Breakfasts, a guest room in a farmhouse that often was attached to the barn, with all its odors. The people were most lovely, charming people. The rooms were always meticulously clean and well appointed. In 1984, the American dollar was at its highest value ever so, a night at a Zimmer frei with "Frühstück"—breakfast of tea and a roll, and egg if you requested—could cost as little as ten American dollars. I rarely spent more the five dollars for a good meal in a quite nice restaurant.

One of the nicest times I had with my children came that summer of 1984. My two kids traveled with their mom to visit me in Salzburg and with a rented car we traveled to Italy, Switzerland, Germany and France. They were ages 13 and 15, perfect ages to enjoy all that the cultures had to offer and not get too bored. We bounced along the streets, enjoying the sites and each other's company. We had a particularly great time in Venice and in Paris. They enjoyed the intrigue of the canals in Venice and the lights of Paris. Although wanting to take them to a nice restaurant in Paris, they preferred McDonalds, which they had missed. We traveled, for the most part on the cheap, staying in some pretty crappy hotels, but we were there. Gina told me, one day, that her good friend asked how we could afford a trip to Europe and I answered that she, Gina, take notice of the difference in the value of our and their furniture. They had new, up to date furniture and we had good, but mostly garage sale specials. It was a matter of priorities.

This was a great education for my kids. One of the highlights or lowlights was a stop in Dachau, Germany, the town of one of the horrible concentration camps. You can study about the atrocities of the Second World War, but nothing prepares you for the reality of seeing the camps. The sign on the entrance still reads; "Arbeit macht frei"—Work makes you free. The first thing you see in the museum are huge blow up photographs of the carnage—dead bodies on piles, skinny, emaciated bodies of people barely alive, and the starkness of the camp. Gina asked, "Dad, how did photographers get in there to take pictures"? When I told her that the Germans themselves took the pictures, she was still a bit mystified. When we left after an hour or so viewing the bunks, the ovens, and the grounds, there was a haunted silence for many miles.

In October, Herr Knoll was scheduled to teach a master class in Porto, Portugal, which he led annually for a number of years. He asked me to travel there to participate in the class. I decided to go, many of my friends had left to return home and I would have been several weeks without voice lessons. And when would I get another chance to go to Portugal?

Porto is a small, poor, coastal city in southern Portugal. It is a very old city, characterized by painted ceramic tiles covering many of the buildings. However, many of them were in severe disrepair. Old, but beautiful wood trolleys traversed the street as public transportation. Poor people lined some of the streets with food for sale, much of it not looking very appetizing—the fish looked bad and smelled worse. I stayed in a rather shabby, inexpensive hotel where the shower was in the middle of the bathroom, so soaked everything in the room when showing.

I flew in around noon, very tired, but thought I would check out the class that had already commenced. There, I met a number of the Portuguese participants and sat beside a nice young woman and struck up a pleasant conversation. Did I mention that Knoll was known as a not too secret skirt chaser? That night, after I was in bed—around 1:00 am, my phone rang to my surprise. It was this young woman, in a frantic voice, telling me that she was frightened—Knoll had drunk a half bottle of Jack Daniels and was sexually threatening her. He had told her to call me—god knows why. I just tried to calm her down and told her to call authorities if necessary. It was my first night in the country, for god's sake.

Apparently, there had been relations between them in the past, but now she wanted none of it. The upshot was that she and I became good friends. She was very kind to me and showed me a lot of Porto and Portuguese life that I otherwise would not have experienced. She took me to the House of Port—yes, port wine is made in Porto. It was beautiful watching the barges with a load of oaken barrels slowly move down the river. The menu at the House of Port contained, probably, one hundred plus types of port. We ordered a sample offering of ten different ports—sweet to dry, light to dark. She took me, for dinner, at her parents' "country club"—not at all fancy, but private.

Everything with Herr Knoll was political and we all wanted him to like us so he would promote us to an agent and to sing in the public recital in Porto. It was dicey, to say the least, to befriend "his girl", that he viewed as betraying him. He thought we were sleeping together and became very jealous. He was mad when he discovered she had taken me to the country club—she had never taken him there.

His great temper boiled over another time when he came to class and the substitute pianist was incompetent. Knoll yelled and screamed, left the class saying he was returning home—which was about half way through the several week course. Oh my, they came to me for help—I guess because I was older and they thought I had some sway over Knoll. I was to plead with him to stay and they promised to always provide a competent accompanist. Six of us—the head of the conservatory, who had sponsored him, my friend, a couple other students and myself—piled into a car and went across the river to where he was staying. I felt in a real bind—not to offend Knoll, but to help these people who had paid good money to bring him to Porto. I don't remember how I did it, but I persuaded him to stay and continue his class.

In November, Herr Knoll was going to Amsterdam to give a similar class, but only for a week. This time, I took an overnight train to Amsterdam to see the sights and study with him. It was a new experience to sleep in a train compartment with two other men and an elderly German woman. The only modesty was being considerate when people changed into their sleeping outfit by looking away.

Amsterdam is another lovely city with all its canals, art museums and concert halls. Highlights of the visit were a wonderful cruise through the canals, a concert in the famous Concertgebouw and spending several hours in the Rijksmuseum.

Preparing for a recital back in Keene, I was studying the Robert Schumann song cycle, *Die Dichterliebe*—the poet's love. For his text, Schumann used the great German writer, Heinrich Heine's poems. In these poems, there are a lot of references to places and things in Germany. I wanted to visit all of them to help me with an understanding of the poems.

I traveled to Heidelberg, where there is a huge wine vat—mentioned in the cycle—that the prince of Heidelberg had connected directly to his banquet room.

A trip up the Rhine, beginning in Meinz provided observation of more mentions in the Heine poems, such as the Meinz Brücke—bridge. The cruise on the Rhine was beautiful, living up to the wonderful vistas you see in publicity. The cruise ended in Köln, one of the great cities of Germany. You can't help but be impressed with one of the greatest cathedrals in the world—third largest and boasts the highest spire that dominates the skyline. The famous shrine of the Three Magi is located there with their buried skulls and clothes. It contains a fine collection of Roman artifacts and some very fine art. A quite large painting, a triptych, that is mentioned in the song cycle almost fills one of the chapels. This was a wonderful first hand experience of relating my travels to my music.

I trained to Vienna a number of times, again very convenient—you could leave Salzburg early in the morning, spend a nice day in the city, jump a train back late the same day. I had a friend who had an audition in Vienna, so I decided to go along and we would see if we could get tickets to the opera. We found out that you could get "standing room only" tickets, if you stood in line at about 2:00 pm before the night's performance. With the good value of the US dollar, these tickets only cost 75 cents. There were actually steps that you sat on at the back of the first balcony, so good "seats". The routine was—after you bought your ticket you rushed to those steps and reserved a spot by tying a scarf or tie around the railing in front of you. The guards were very strict about maintaining that honor system.

After the opera, we decided to go to a Ratskeller—bar—next to the opera house. There were several tables of rowdy men drinking—we found out they were vacuum sweeper salesmen attending a convention—laughing, singing loudly and we joined in when we could, even if we didn't know the words, like the Blue Danube waltz.

As we were leaving, they asked us who we were and we told them "opera singers"—in Europe that is always respected, by all status of people. Well, they begged us to sit down and sing. They called over two musicians who were performing traditional German songs, one playing a wheezy accordion and the other a guitar, and asked us to sing. We were dubious of the guys accompanying us, but the salesmen said sing a few bars and they'll catch on. So one of us launched into an aria and the guys tried to chord along with us. I have never before or since sung Mozart arias with such an accompaniment. The salesmen, though, were so pleased, bought us more wine and we all stumbled out of the joint, as they were sweeping up the bar to close. It wouldn't have happened in the States. We probably would have been run out of the bar if we sang opera.

Those six months in Europe were filled with absolutely life changing experiences, musically, personally and spiritually. I heard many great performances—the great baritone, Herman Prey in the München Opera House, operas and recitals in the renown Salzburg music festival, including a another recital Dietrich Fischer-Dieskau, the opera, *Lucia di Lammermoor* in the beautiful Vienna opera house, chamber music in the old fortress in Salzburg that sits conspicuously on the hill by the city and many other old venues, visited the graves and homes of a number of famous composers, heard some of the great masses in their intended venues, magnificent cathedrals.

Cathedrals were an anathema to our Mennonite humble thinking about what Christ stood for. Mom often said, in derision, how that money would feed so many hungry people. But, I found myself drawn to the beauty, grandeur and majesty of the many cathedrals I visited—large and small. The artwork and sculptures were inspiring. I went many times into the great Dom of Salzburg for quiet meditation—I didn't attempt to pray, not really knowing anymore what prayer was or meant. But the time there did give me a sense of a "Holy Other", a power beyond myself. As mentioned, any time there were candles, I lit one and stood silently for a bit, thinking of Daddy.

I learned how to fend for myself in a completely new environment and culture. My sense of self grew tremendously—learning, on my own, to make friends, to travel, to speak a foreign language, to go to the local markets. I improved as a competent, confident singer and learned more about vocal technique. Without family and academic responsibilities I was able to concentrate on my craft as an artist and performer. Having to sing every day in the summer class forced me to learn music much more quickly and strengthened my voice.

Back in Keene 1985

I HAD A DIFFICULT TIME assimilating back into the American culture, to the family, and to academe. I was so free, in Europe, absorbing all I could. I had to adjust back to the responsibility of job and family.

The professional void was filled with my preparation toward conducting the *Carmina Burana*. Before I left for Europe, I took an opportunity to program my first great masterwork with orchestra and soloists, a goal I had striven for since graduate school. The year 1985 was the college's 75th year anniversary. Grants were available to sponsor large events that highlighted one of the colleges' programs as a part of the celebration. The music department hadn't proposed any ideas for such an event, so I viewed it as an opportunity to perform a large, splashy work with help from some grants. What would be huge and splashy, and draw a lot of attention?

I hit on the idea of performing Orff's *Carmina Burana*. Regardless of its salacious text, it was a big, impressive crowd pleaser. Was I up to the conducting challenges of this work? It demands a large orchestra, lots of percussion, many meter changes, and an understanding of the text. The only piece, with a large Romantic orchestra that I conducted, to that point, was the Brahms *Schickalslied* at Hope College. I checked out a copy of the full score of the *Carmina*, from the library and studied it intensely. Even though it was very complicated, there was nothing in the score that I didn't understand, that with more study and practice I couldn't conduct. So I took the leap, applied for a grant and began six months of studying the score.

It involved a lot of logistical problems and decisions—organizing the orchestra, hiring the ringers for the orchestra and the professional vocal soloists. I invited the Keene Chorale, other singers from the city and college communities to give us enough voices to produce the quality and volume of sound needed.

When the concert time came, it was a thrill to step on the podium and bring this baby to birth. The power of the baton came surging into my body and spirit. The sound permeated my old system—the work became mine.

It was a huge success. As a part of the anniversary celebration, the College President, Vice President, members of the Board of Trustees were among the thrilled audience members. We received very good reviews in a number of the area newspapers.

Keene Sentinel: "Under Lehman's excellent direction, they produced an authentic, idiomatic performance of Orff's work" "He led the cantata with the requisite vigorous vulgarity, but he also brought lightness and wit to it.

Leisure Weekly: "Throughout, there are pervasive, powerful, ever changing rhythms. It was in mastering these rhythm and making them his own that Lehman excelled ".

In the summer of 1985, after such a great sabbatical in 1984, I was looking for something to maintain the enthusiasm with which I returned from Europe. I had seen advertised, many times, the Workshop that the choral icon, Robert Shaw, conducted at Westminster Choir College each summer.

The focused works, that year, were two of the giants among choral masterworks: Bach's *Mass in b minor* and Beethoven's *Missa Solemnis*. I sent in an audition tape and was accepted to participate as a choral singer. We were about 120 good musicians and singers, most of us professional, but we still rehearsed five hours each day for a week to prepare for a concert at the Riverside Presbyterian Church in New York City, on Sunday afternoon.

The second week, we prepared the Beethoven. Shaw's exposés on the works, during rehearsals, inspired and enlightened. He talked about the text and what the two very different composers brought to the music. He talked about their lives, their personalities and their struggles.

I came to believe Shaw identified more with the struggling life of Beethoven than that of the devout Bach. Shaw described what he believed was the spiritual ambivalence of Beethoven in some of the movements of the Mass; particularly how he ends the work with many cries of "Kyrie Eleison" "Have mercy". That powerful setting by Beethoven caused me to falter in tears several times, during the performance of the *Missa Solemnis*.

I would love to have conducted both of those works, but I never felt I had a chorus that could do justice to them. However, the opportunity to sing under Robert Shaw's baton was extremely fortunate and led me to another pinnacle of the interaction of spirituality and music.

My normal life stopped in October 1985 when Mom experienced a severe heart attack and was taken to the hospital. I rushed to Pennsylvania to be by her side, as did my siblings. She was conscious and somewhat alert. She said to each of us, some unusual words that weren't characteristic of her—Mom could be quite critical. My hair was styled in a curly perm and I had a full beard. She reached up, touched my beard and said, "Carroll, I like your hair". I knew, in real life, she didn't like my hair. She told Alta she liked her dress and teased Wilmer that his bright red and white-stripped shirt was too flashy for an old man—he wasn't that old.

The vigil of waiting for death was an interesting revelation of life and death for me. I kept a journal of those days, which helped me deal with the pain. I realized how short life is, how dying can be a struggle even when spiritually prepared to go.

Mom often told the story of watching her father die, of his seeing bright lights and hearing singing. To her it was evidence of his entering the "Pearly Gates" of Heaven. I think she always wanted to leave this world in that glorious manner, but it didn't happen that way—the body struggled and then relaxed and she simply slipped away. When she passed in the morning October 3, 1985, Alta and I watched the heart monitor count down to zero. Alta remembered that it was my parent's wedding anniversary and we wished them Happy Anniversary. We firmly believe she held on to life to die on that day. After Daddy died, she often spoke of being lonely, missing her love of 47 years, and wanting to go to meet him. We children believe that that loneliness and desire brought death only a year and a half after Daddy died.

With a heavy heart, realizing that I at the age of 43 and was not the last generation of my family, I turned to music. With the success of the *Carmina Burana*, I organized the KSC Oratorio Society. My goal was to perform a major work every two years, so that a student could experience two works in their four years of study. We performed the Haydn *Creation* as our next offering, a run of Requiems—those by Verdi, Brahms, Fauré, and Mozart. I told people that I really didn't have a death wish, or a fatalistic attitude, but Requiems seemed to provide a palette for the best work for some composers.

My greatest goal was to, sometime, somehow, fulfill my dream of conducting the Verdi *Requiem*. In 1989 I took the leap and planned for a performance of it by the Oratorio Society. This time I invited the Nashua Choral Society to join us. I begged until the resident Apple Hill Chamber Players were required to sit 1st chair strings, asked adjunct professors to play first chair of the wind and brass sections and to choose one of their talented students to sit next to them. I invited a few good, local players and hired a few professional players to augment our KSC Chamber Orchestra.

I wanted fine, appropriate soloists for this maybe once in a lifetime experience. The solos in the *Requiem* are grand and demanding—very operatic and are some of the highlights of the entire work. I went to the Dean pleading for money to hire professional soloists. Even though he was a musician, an instrumentalist, he didn't understand the necessity of the request, was very resistant and wondered why I couldn't use local soloists. I became upset and told him that it was so important to me that I would write out a check for two thousand dollars that he could cash if I couldn't raise it. He scoffed at the idea, but I was very serious. I had no way of knowing if I would ever conduct this special work again and it would be worth $2000, of my own money, to have great soloists. I had no way on knowing that in the next week, I received notice that an anonymous donor had given $1500 toward the performance, which was close enough.

I called the director of Opera North, a good friend, and asked for recommendations for soloists. He highly recommended soprano, Susan Owen, who sang in a Verdi opera for him. I called her and she accepted, and recommended a young tenor, Francisco Casanova, from the Dominican Republic with whom she had recently sung Verdi's opera, *Rigoletto*—which has similar arias as the Requiem. I called him and he was on board. I called an old friend, Peter Tiboris in NYC and he recommended a bass from upstate New York. I hired a graduate student, mezzo-soprano, from New England Conservatory and the cast was in place.

In the middle of the performance, I really had to control my emotions as the music was filling my soul more than any other work I had conducted to that point. I had listened to it hundreds of times, dreaming of conducting it. Although a Catholic requiem, with a very different concept of death and the afterlife than for the Mennonite boy with shit on his boots, far from the gospel songs of yore, I was filled with the awe of it all and swept into some ethereal feelings.

Every moment affected my nervous system—the Dies Irae with its loud syncopated pounding of the bass drum and the screaming choral motive which so severely pictures the "Day of Judgment", the "Day of Wrath", to the plaintive theme of the Hostia, to the last chanted, almost whispered, whimper of the Libera me. We gave two performances to great acclaim and I am proud to say that Susan and Francisco both went on to fine careers, including singing at the Metropolitan Opera, but I have lost track of the other two.

Since the Nashua Choral Society performed with us, we received a review from the music critic of the Nashua Telegraph, who I was told was usually quite critical of performances, but he wrote:

"Under the baton of Carroll J. Lehman the performance was powerful, rich, warmly romantic, fully expressive of Verdi's growing concern with death, and the doubt and hope therein".

In the summer of 1986, I returned to Europe with my brother, Nelson. We inherited about $25,000 each and the family was discussing, one day, what we would do with it. Nelson complained that he would just pay bills, and we all encouraged him to do something special for himself. I suggested he go to Europe with me—he always had wanted to see the Alps and other European sights. I wanted to study a short time again with Herr Knoll.

Nelson and I spent about 10 days traveling in Germany, Austria and Northern Italy. It became one of the great memories in our relationship and it's even more special now that Nelson passed in March 2015. We got along very well traveling together for brothers who fought like cats and dogs, when young.

One story I love to tell on Nelson and he didn't mind. We had rented a car at the airport and were going to head for Salzburg. It was a very hot day and I decided to stop at the English gardens in Munich. I told Nelson it was like Central Park in New York City and he would enjoy it. I was quite sure that there would be some naked people around, as I described earlier, but I didn't tell him. I parked the car and we entered the gardens over a small bridge. I noticed that there were some young things sunbathing nude down by the stream. All of a sudden, Nelson noticed and exclaimed; "Oh, my god, do you see that? There are girls down there without any clothes on". I said; "Nah, really"? And laughed my head off.

I can't describe all that I experienced and learned each time I visited Europe. The concerts and operas I attended, the people I met, the education, formal and informal that I received, the culture I learned to deeply enjoy.

When our American politics gets so bad, at times, I often say if I were younger I would move to Germany or Austria. Their system of health care, local and cross-country transportation, history, sophisticated culture, often beckons. One example, as mentioned: as they are building bigger, faster trains, we are tearing up our tracks for people to ride snowmobiles.

Beyond the European trip, I wanted to do something special with my bit of inheritance, as well. Learning to fly a plane was another goal high on my bucket list. One of my Lancaster Mennonite roommates learned to fly soon after our graduation. He bought a small two-seater plane and would fly up from Lancaster, on a summer Sunday afternoons to visit. We would fly over the Chambersburg area and my farm, and I wanted so badly to learn to fly. Of course as, with any risky adventure, Mom was desperately opposed.

With some of that inheritance money, I decided now was the time to become a pilot. I took lessons with an excellent instructor and when I landed after my first solo flight, I gave homage to Mom with a fist pump. I really enjoyed flying my rented Cessna 150 over the Monadnock region. It was a thrill to make my first, and only, cross-country solo flight from Keene to Glen Falls, NY, some 100 miles. I flew just under some wonderful fluffy clouds, across Mt. Snow and into Glen Falls. The head wind was so strong going west; I saw cars on the highway below speeding along faster than me. Of course, coming back East with the tail wind, I traveled the distance in half the time.

I loved challenges, but I was committed to experiencing them only if I could afford them, they remained fun and they didn't endanger my life. Even though I was very close to achieving my private pilot's license—which meant I could carry passengers and could fly farther than 50 miles from Keene airport without permission of my instructor—I decided it was time to quit.

My money was running out, my marriage was in trouble, which caused me to be distracted, so I walked away. But to this day I can feel what it was like to lift off of the runway and to land the plane back there.

Monadnock Chorus 1989

SOON AFTER COMING TO KEENE, I attended a performance by the Monadnock Chorus (MC) of the *Messiah*, with orchestra and soloists. MC was/is an amateur, regional chorus of about 100 members, based in Peterborough, NH. It was not a great performance but I thought, if the opportunity arose, I would strongly seek the directorship, since their mission was to perform some of the great masterworks with orchestra, my dream. I appeared with them as a soloist in several works, including the Bach *Magnificat* and Handel's *Israel in Egypt*.

In fall of 1982, the conductor and music director took a sabbatical, and invited me to guest conduct. I really enjoyed the experience and, again, coveted that position. That director retired from the chorus in 1989, and I intensely sought the position. I was invited to an interview and to conduct a trial rehearsal.

That fall, I was hired to be the music director and conductor of the Monadnock Chorus. This became the beginning of a 20-year tenure with them, an association that provided me with some of my most wonderful experiences of music, travel and social acquaintances.

In those first years with the Monadnock Chorus, I strove to improve the quality of all areas of the performances. The orchestra was constituted of mainly amateur musicians from the area, with a few professional ringers for the concerts. The local players required weekly rehearsals to learn the music, but some of the needed rarer played instruments—oboes, French horns, bassoons—were hired professionals who just came in for the last couple of rehearsals. So rehearsals with just the amateurs were a challenge, inefficient and I felt a waste of time. I wanted a skilled orchestra that could rehearse three times before a concert and perform. I had the unpleasant task to inform the weaker, local players that their services were not needed, and the first chair players that I was going to hire professionals for those positions. Gradually I replaced all the unpaid players with professionals, and only hired the locals that were capable of meeting my desired level of performance quality.

The next challenge was to hire, high-level professional soloists. I was very fortunate to have some wonderful boards that supported my ideas of improvement, for the most part. I had to convince them that we would need to pay better stipends for excellent soloists.

One of my arguments was, and still is, that people have to pay plumbers $70 an hour, but only want to pay professional musicians—who had spent a large amount of money on education and training—less than $25 an hour. I gradually increased players' and soloists' fees enough that fine musicians would perform with us. Even if it still wasn't the amount they deserved, they enjoyed coming to the Monadnock Region, singing and playing with our gracious chorus members, our deeply appreciative audiences, the choice of literature, my conducting skills and the passion that I brought to the performances.

We undertook and performed to acclaim some of the greatest music in the world including the Beethoven *Ninth Symphony*, the Verdi *Requiem*, the Anton Dvorak and Gioachino Rossini *Stabat Maters*, the *Carmina Burana*, Gerschwin's *Rhapsody in Blue*, and J. S. Bach's *Christmas Oratorio*. You can see the full list in the back of this book.

Special themed programs of Christmas music always thrilled the chorus and the audiences. We performed a Russian Christmas singing the Rachmaninoff *Vespers*, with a former Russian born student of mine, Anton Belov, as coach and soloist. Another favorite was a Latin American Christmas with my good friend, Maria Guinand from Venezuela, whom I invited for a week residency as coach and conductor of traditional Latin carols. The most enthusiastic program was an African-American Christmas. Geoff Hicks, from Boston, a superb musician, pianist and singer, schooled us in several of his selected pieces. His energy, his gift of improvising at the piano and singing had the audience on their feet, clapping, dancing, and crying as they sang along with us.

Italy, Germany, and Austria 1991

WITH A GROUP OF THE Monadnock Chorus members, I led four overseas trips, experiencing great people, music and venues. Our first trip occurred in 1991 with a tour to Europe—Austria, Italy and Germany. This experience would have been the apex of my career had I not been fortunate enough to have many more.

We sang in some of the greatest cathedrals in Italy. We sang at a weekday Mass at the Il Duomo di Firenze—The Dome of Florence. The organ was quite some distance from the choir and it was a challenge not to conduct the reverberation—which was about five seconds—instead of the live production of sound. I had to wait for the reverb at the end of a phrase, before launching into the next section. We only had about ten minutes in the space before the Mass began. Next, we traveled to Rome to participate in Sunday High Mass in the main nave of St. Peter's Cathedral. It was an amazing experience, musically and spiritually. All the history of the Basilica with St Peter's Tomb present, the great organ, a full congregation and all the ritual invoked total emotional and spiritual moments.

I learned quickly about how hallow this great Basilica is and the respect it engenders. In anticipation of singing for Masses, I included, in our repertoire, a number of choral settings of parts of the Mass—a "Kyrie', a "Gloria", "Agnus Dei" among them. We sang them in Florence without any objection. But before the service at St. Peters, they wanted to inspect our music to judge its appropriateness. We were not informed that only Gregorian chant was permitted in the High Mass in the Basilica, and we didn't have any prepared. I made the dumb observation that our repertoire was acceptable in the Duomo in Florence. The young clergy answered with some indignity, "BUT THIS IS THE BASCILICA". So, during the Mass the young clergy stood in front of us and intoned the chant—it was simple and we would repeat it. Although the Pope was not there, the many present Roman Church hierarchy created an impressive tableau. Whether not Catholic, or not even Christian, the impression of that great historic cathedral and its rites speaks to ones deep spiritual needs. I took communion, because it seemed that my deep, overwhelming, sacred, spiritual emotions, of the moment, demanded it.

Rob Holden, a former student of mine, and soloist for the trip, sang "Panis Angelicus" during communion and tears dribbled down many of our cheeks. I have seldom felt such a presence of a "Holy Other" than at that moment. As the Mass ended, our organist played a grandiose, composition by Heinrich Schütz with full-blown pipes filling the nave with thunderous sounds. At the end the audience, enraptured, began to clap but the clergy quickly hushed them.

The following day, through a contact of one of our chorus members, we were invited to the Pope's weekly Vatican radio broadcast. We were among about 500 attendees, some in groups like us—a group of children from South America, a group of nuns, and various important individuals. The Monsignor from the region of the group and/or individuals introduced them to the Pope. After our introduction, we performed for the Pope. I chose the Bruckner *Ave Maria*, a beautiful, flowing, eight-part a cappella work. The Pope nodded and hand gestured his approval. After his broadcast homily, he came through the audience to meet the people. I was fortunate to have a stand next to the aisle. As he came by, he took my hand and we peered into each other's eyes for a moment and I felt, again, a "Holy" presence.

This was another amazing ride, far distant from my Mennonite roots, which viewed Catholics' salvation suspect, where the wealth to create a Basilica was scoffed at and the rituals of the Mass were misunderstood. It was an unexpected turn in my spiritual journey to experience that awe and holiness.

Next, we traveled to the famed St Mark's Cathedral in Venice—a cathedral inseparable from its influence on, what came to be historically called Venetian polychoral, antiphonal school of choral music. The cathedral, with its interior, styled in a Greek cross and its several choir lofts, was the setting for many compositions by Andrea and Giovanni Gabrieli and Claudio Monteverdi. I was disappointed that we didn't sing for a High Mass in the main nave, but in one of the many chapels located in the wings. This was January and the Cathedral was damp and cold, we wore our coats and as we sang, steam emanated from our mouths. After the service, we were allowed to move into the main nave, separate into groups and experience the antiphonal effect of Gabrieli and succeeding composers.

That day, the news arrived that the U.S. was threatening to engage in war with Iraq, to push it out of Kuwait, which it had invaded. As we emerged from our performance in St. Mark's, we saw a circle of Italian people surrounding the parameter of the Square, holding signs and candles, protesting the U. S. going to war. A number of us felt compelled to join them, to show our solidarity with their sentiment. The Italians were profoundly moved with that gesture of peace

We took an overnight train from Venice to Vienna. It was an endurance issue for some of us. The question the next morning, when we arrived was, "Were you in the heated or the unheated cars"? Several of the cars were unheated and the thin paper blankets handed out by the train personnel didn't help keep out the January cold for us in the unheated cars.

We sang at Sunday Mass in the Votivkirche, a beautiful neo-Gothic cathedral located on the Ringstrasse in Vienna. It was difficult to enjoy the beauty when you were shivering. As in St. Mark's, it was cold and bleak; we wore our overcoats to keep warm and as the chorus sang, steam again poured out of their mouths.

The next stop was Dachau, Germany. I had mixed feelings about visiting Dachau, again. If you remember I took my kids there in 1984. But the Monadnock Chorus had an exchange program with the Dachau Tafelmusik Chor—table music chorus—a community chorus similar to us. They had a relationship of visiting each other before I became director. The Monadnock

Chorus had visited them some years before and the Tafelmusik Chor had visited the MC in Peterborough one summer.

We were invited to stay in Chor members' homes rather than hotels. It was very interesting what different attitudes, in relationship to the Dachau Concentration Camp, our chorus members experienced with their hosts. Some hosts wanted to avoid it, others took their guests, dropped them off expressing deep regret for that sad history but felt Americans should visit it, and still others just seemed to accept it as a terrible time in the town's history.

We shared a joint concert with the Chor, each performed some of their repertoire and we sang a couple of songs together—one of their choosing and one of our choosing. Each conductor conducted his group's choice. Many of the Tafelmusik members spoke very little English, but I was able to conduct most of the rehearsal in German, giving very short phrase instructions, not worrying about proper grammar, etc.

Afterwards they had arranged for a great party, starting with the breaking of the "bung"--a corklike stopper that seals the keg while the beer seasons. A lot of beer flowed and the conversation got quite lively.

The downer for us that evening was the announcement that the U.S. was, indeed, going to war with Iraq. It was interesting that many of the Germans supported it because they felt that the U.S. was their liberator in WW II and that now, that was the intent of the U.S. again—to liberate, this time, Kuwait. It was a different perspective to ruminate about.

The next day we were scheduled to return home from Frankfort. We were informed that the Frankfurt airport could possibly be a target of terrorists. When we arrived the airport looked like a city under siege. Tanks surrounded the terminal—inside many soldiers with menacing looking automatic army rifles patrolled the crowd. We were told, by our leaders, to not look like American tourists—of course we had backpacks, camera bags, suitcases and only spoke English.

That first overseas music tour was the first of six overseas trips, each having its unique experiences and influence in my life.

New York City 1991

IN 1991, I RECEIVED MY second sabbatical—this time I proposed living in New York City, taking some classes at Columbia University, and take in what NYC had to offer—concerts, operas, museums, etc. I had developed an interest in vocal therapy, which is different from voice teaching—it deals more with the rehabilitation of a troubled voice, rather than building a healthy voice.

I had attended many conferences, over the years, on the subject—mainly associated with the Voice Foundation—a group of otolaryngologists, voice scientists, voice teachers, speech and vocal therapists—read many articles and books on the topics, most edited or written by the brilliant medical doctor and performing baritone, Dr. Robert Sokoloff.

Several otolaryngologists recommended patients to me; some were amateur singers, some people who were recovering from vocal fold surgery, and professional people who used their speaking voice a great deal. One such person was a high school teacher, who lost her voice some 30 days a year from laryngitis. I worked with her for about 6 months, teaching her proper breath support and control, to place the voice higher in pitch and in resonance, and omit glottal stops—explosive onsets of a sound. The last I had contact with her, she hadn't lost any days of school, unless an illness affected her voice.

Although I was knowledgeable about the anatomy of the voice, I was not as educated about the pathology of the voice. Thus, I arranged to take a number of classes directed toward speech pathologists at Columbia University in NYC on my sabbatical. I consulted by phone with a highly respected professor, I knew from the Voice Foundation and we determined the classes best suited for me with my background and goals.

I arranged to stay at the Menno House, run by the Mennonite Church, in NYC while I searched for an apartment I could afford. I found a studio apartment on the Upper East Side and leased it for 4 months.

One of my first days in NYC, I met with my Columbia advisor, the one who arranged my classes. He looked on the schedule of classes and said, "Oh my god, I teach those classes in the spring". I was disappointed, because none of the classes taught in the fall would benefit me, since I didn't have sufficient background in speech pathology to understand the material.

But, I had my sabbatical and my apartment, so there were not many options. I kept a practice room at Columbia, where I could sing several times a week. I was able to get last minute tickets, at highly discounted prices, to many concerts in Carnegie Hall, Lincoln Center, operas at the Met and musicals on Broadway. I attended concerts and services in some of the great cathedrals—including St. John's and St. Patrick's. I attended several voice master classes, including one led by Pavarotti.

Even though I had visited NYC many times, this indeed was a whole different experience, to live in the city and each day walk the streets, observe the people and feel the hustle and bustle. It was a time when you couldn't walk a couple of blocks without being confronted by a panhandler seeking money. It so disturbed me that I had to decide how I could deal with it. So on numerous occasions when I bought a bagel for breakfast or a sandwich for lunch, I bought an extra one and handed that to the beggar. I decided to take an individual under my wings and concentrate on helping him. So almost daily I would take him something or give him a little money. He barely responded, and then I realized that he, as were many of the homeless I observed, was severely mentally or emotionally handicapped, and I couldn't fix that.

In the end that sabbatical, in many ways fulfilled the real intent of a sabbatical—to return to KSC refreshed, rejuvenated and inspired with new vigor and ideals. The farm boy went to the city—another great motorcycle ride!

The eighties and nineties were a time of self-discovery along with a developing family. My children were growing and thriving in many areas. Scott was becoming a fine violinist, having studied since the age of 6. Gina tried violin lessons in Washington, and piano lessons in Keene, but neither stuck, she took to ballet lessons.

In Scott's freshman year in Keene public school, Scott was fed up with his social life and academic life. He wanted to transfer to a private school and begin anew.

New England is known for its great private schools, but they are very expensive and I had idealistic problems with some of the best students leaving the public school system. His mother was stronger about the possibilities and we went to several for interviews. It was eye popping for this farm boy to see the process of the uppity schools. We were interviewed as much, or more, than the student. We had no pedigree—graduation from an Ivy League school or even parents who had a college education, for instance.

We chose Northfield-Mt. Herman School just 30 minutes from Keene, which has the most practical approach to education—every student works for an hour every day, students who came from many countries, a well-rounded curriculum with classes involving sexually, world religion, ethics and world peace. The great evangelist, D.L. Moody, an icon to my evangelist Grandpa Shank, founded Northfield. It was established with a very fundamentalist dogma. It now had morphed into a non-sectarian school, but maintained that religious influence. Scott roomed in the dormitory there and thrived. Gina attended there her last three years, as well.

These were some rugged times for me—my marriage broke apart and I moved into an apartment in Troy, NH. It had four comfortable rooms on the second floor of an old New England colonial house—my entrance was up the center staircase. I did become happy there, with my yellow tabby cat, Morris, sorting out my life and wondering what the future would hold. I learned to be comfortable with being alone. It was a time of reflection and searching my inner core. I sought to put all my fifty years of life into some perspective,

In 1993, I remarried and bought a former farmhouse, with a lot of history, in the quaint little town of Hancock. I enjoyed having about two and one half acres, mostly in grass, but I was able to till a large spot for a garden. The barn had burned down many years ago—what was left was the first floor that now served as a three bay storage shed for my little Miata and a lot of stuff.

Musically I continued to seek experiences that would educate and inspire me. At the Robert Shaw Workshop in 1985, I became friends with a number of choral directors and one, in particular, who said that to really understand J. S. Bach, I should attend the Oregon Bach Festival in Eugene, Oregon under the directorship of Helmut Rilling. The summer of 1992, with development money granted by KSC, I headed out to be enlightened

For the next five years, I attended the Festival, four as a conducting auditor and one as an active conducting student. I can't express on paper how these experiences thrilled every part of my being. The first year during the unbelievable performance of the Bach, St. John's Passion, I pitied the person beside me, as I wept many, many times. The soloists responded to Rilling's passion and gave incredible renderings of the characters the likes of Jesus, John, Pilate and the emotional arias.

Over the years, Rilling allowed us to peer into his passion, his musicianship—he conducted everything from memory—his spiritually, his kind personhood. His quiet demeanor belied the wealth of insights into the great music that he learned over the years of study. In the afternoon concert lecture series, Helmut explained the work to be presented conducted by the active participants in the conducting class. He opined on the historical, musical and spiritual perspectives

The Festival Chorus was made up of professional singers from around the country. The orchestra contained some of the best players, not only in the states, but a number that Rilling brought from Europe. Their level of performance was genius—I had never heard such virtuosic performances on difficult instruments like the oboe, English horn and French horn. The festival program not only involved some of the greatest presentations of the works of Bach I had ever heard, but many other memorable works. They premiered a number of Arvo Pert's works and other contemporary composers. I heard the Dvorak *Stabat Mater*, live, for the first time and it became one of my favorite works.

Helmut was always aware of world events and history. In the year of the 50th anniversary of the end of WWII, choruses from East Germany, Japan and Germany were brought together to perform the Britten War Requiem—a work with the traditional Latin movements intertwined with movements on the poems of British writer, Wilfred Owens, who served and was killed in WW I. The concert was endowed with deep emotions from within the individuals whose countries were fighting each other 50 years ago.

A wealthy sponsor of the Festival entertained a huge party on their ranch, after the concert. To see and feel the pathos engendered by the music just sung, that interjected the social event with friendship and love, brought home many good human qualities.

The last year that I attended the Festival, I decided to subject myself to being a student conductor. Through audition tapes and videos, I was selected to conduct part of the Bach *Christmas Oratorio*. It was nerve racking at first, to stand before these amazing musicians, even though I was very experienced and was, by far, the oldest in the class. Helmut was very kind and supportive of my conducting style and insights. To conduct those super musicians, was another highlight of my career.

Russia, Latvia, Estonia 1992

IN 1992, I RECEIVED A call from the New Hampshire Friendship Chorus, inviting me to conduct them on their second tour, this time to Russia. I didn't know much about the chorus, but jumped at the chance. The New Hampshire Friendship Chorus (NHFC) was organized for the express purpose of making concert tours to various countries to interact with the people, to better understand their culture, and share concerts with their musical ensembles. Their motto is "Making Music and Making Friends".

I led this group on three unforgettable tours. The members of the chorus came from all walks of life, of various levels of musicianship and quality of voices to rehearse a program, of largely American music, that I had chosen. We met every couple of weeks—about 10 times-- to rehearse and plan for the trip. What great anticipation I had for this trip! Not only would we visit Russia, but Tallinn, Estonia and Riga, Latvia,

Boris Yeltsin had just stood in front of the "White House" in Moscow and declared Russia as a different country with more openness in government, a freer press and a government serving the people. But, the economy went bust, and it was a desperate time for the people. We saw long lines at grocery markets for the few items of food remaining on their shelves. People stood on the sides of streets and bridges selling what little they had—a pair of shoes, glass tumblers, little bits of jewelry, a couple items of clothing. Everyone looked disheartened, weathered and sad.

In one town, as I was about to board the bus, when a mother begged me to take her beautiful young daughter—maybe sixteen or so—with me so she could have a better life. She said that the daughter was well trained and would be very good to me. So sad.

In Moscow, our first stop, we performed a concert in an abandoned church—like most churches were during the Soviet reign—with an excellent chamber choir. Most people that we interacted with spoke very little or no English, but we learned to communicate with hand gestures or through our guides' translations. We were received with open arms, the "cold war" all but forgotten. We had been told of the Russians' fondness for gifts, giving and receiving, so we came prepared with gifts of American jeans, candy, and small souvenirs from New England. They gave us small Russian souvenirs.

I was viewed as the "maestro" from America. The flowers after the concerts kept coming, fresh beautiful bouquets that I left for the maids in our hotels.

In Leningrad, just renamed back to St. Petersburg, after the concert we were treated to an all-night ride through the canals of the city—much like Amsterdam—with our host choir. In the beginning of July, it never became fully dark. The conductor and I communicated well through gestures, inflections, and vodka. I had purchased a flask of Smirnoff, in some small store and when I pulled out the bottle, he exclaimed "Smirnoff". When I had some of their "rotgut" vodka, I knew why. We sipped from paper cups most of the night and were quite good, happy friends by the time we arrived at the dock—about 5:00 am.

To reach Estonia and Latvia, we rode an overnight train to Estonia. Small compartments with bunks served as our bedrooms for three or four people. In the middle of the night, if we were lucky enough to be sleeping, we were awakened with loud angry Russians talking outside the halted train.

Our guide informed us that we were stopped at the Estonian/Russian border for visa checks. The Russians on board did not have visas, because they still viewed the Baltic States as a part of a Soviet Union. But the Estonians had recently declared that everyone, including Russians, needed a visa to enter their borders. The Border Police blocked them from entering their country and the Russians were stuck in the middle of the night, at a tiny train station in the middle of nowhere.

When we told this story to the Estonians, they deemed it humorous and what the Russians deserved for not respecting their sovereignty. For the first time in years, Estonia was free. They had just had their first democratic elections, minted their own money and defended their borders.

In the capital city, Tallinn, we sang with a community chorus in the open air of a museum with old, historic buildings—their Williamsburg. A new beer had been brewed for the occasion and cured in a wood keg. The bung was removed, and we drank with pleasure. More people spoke English with this group and we had a delightful time.

A bus trip took us to Riga, the capital city of Latvia. What a beautiful city situated on a hill with many towers as you view the city from the top of one of those hills. Artists with easels painting various scenery and flower merchants displaying their beautiful bouquets in kiosks lined many of the streets. Horses and carriages would take you for a ride around the city on its cobblestone streets.

We sang with two choirs, one a community choir similar to ours, and the other a smaller more talented chamber choir. They both sang with great enthusiasm, inspired by singing for Americans. The chamber choir sang a Spiritual "Every time I feel the Spirit" and a jazz piece, trying to imitate the style of each. One member had obviously listened to jazz and African-Americans singers. He did a very creditable job of aping them, looked for—and received—our applause of approval.

Both groups vied for our attention, but we spent more time with the community group, most like us. The director of that group and I spent some time together discussing many things in German which for both of us was our best second language. After the concert, we were invited into a number of the members' homes in small apartments. I crowded into one with several of our chorus members and appreciated their great effort to show us their hospitality. They provided a nice meal and much friendship.

We celebrated the 4th of July with them involving great festivities, into which had gone a lot of planning and energy. We were ushered into a beautiful park with a small chapel. They came in their native garb carrying American and Latvian flags. There was a short program in the chapel with a deep feeling of their respect for our independence, settled so long ago, while they were attempting to find their own.

I always tried to find the national anthem of all the countries we were to visit, a symbol of respect, that the people truly appreciated. In my research, I found the Latvian national anthem. But we learned that during the Soviet rule, they were not permitted to sing it. So, they adopted a very beautiful ballad that they used metaphorically to describe their plight.

It tells of a sailor that sets out to sea with his lover left behind. He doesn't know when he will be able to return, but speaks of his faithfulness to her. It is a short piece with many verses and they taught it to us. When we all gathered on stage after the formal concert and after their gifts and many, many flowers—the grand piano's top was loaded with beautiful bouquets—we linked arms and while swaying, sang it repeatedly, humming it when we didn't know the words, with the shedding of some tears. It was another amazing moment of my life, people meeting people with love and respect, joining together through music.

Russia still maintained an air force base in Latvia and the Latvians were strongly disturbed by Russian planes flying over their country. The mayor passionately pleaded with us to return to America and strongly seek support from our government to get the Russians out of their sovereign country. Patriotism weld up in my body and soul like never before. Living in a Democracy, with all its imperfections, became more sacred to me. I respected the struggle it took to gain our own freedom and independence.

More great moments awaited us as we flew into the heart of Siberia to the cities of Novosibirsk and Irkutsk. Our concert in Irkutsk was scheduled with a male choir. We all had looked forward to hearing and singing with a sample of the great Russian men's chorus tradition, so well known for their big choral sound, anchored by those deep Russian basses. But, it fell through at the last moment—as was typical of Russian schedules—and we were rerouted to meet with a group some hours from the city.

As we climbed aboard an old bus, similar to our school busses, most of us complained and the complaints became more frequent as we bumped along for about four hours over roads that contained deep potholes and cracked pavement.

We arrived at a little town, deep into southern Siberia. Being in the middle of the summer, the heat was stifling. Townspeople, in traditional costumes, greeted us and we moved into a small town hall for a concert. The traditional salt bread ritual welcome seemed like taking communion. A round loaf of bread with a scoop out of the middle filled with salt was passed around and we tore off a small chunk, dipped it in the salt and eat it. They sang a number of their folksongs and we performed songs in our repertoire that were American folk songs.

After the short concert, our bus was driven down to a small river. A reception was planned for us, but it was across the river in a cow pasture. Fording the shallow river was the only way to get there, so pants legs and skirts, alike, were jacked up and off we went. Many of the Russian men came prepared with speedo swimsuits under their trousers and they stripped down immediately. As the heat became more intense a number of the men took off their shirts.

Soon after arriving, a young thing grabbed me by the arm and pulled me down the bank, into the river, wearing all my clothes, shoes, and watch. I was so soaked, so after we climbed back up the bank, I stripped my shirt off as well.

Long heavy paper sheets lay in rows on the ground where the food was served. The meal included large pickled mushrooms, a fish soup—the fish heads with eyes poking up through the liquid—that was said to have been caught that morning, Pepsi and, of course vodka—"rot gut" vodka.

Several men became pretty happy from the vodka, including me. My excuse was that every time I turned around someone wanted to offer a toast, my being the maestro. The mayor offered the most emotional toast. He said, through a translator, with tears welling up in his eyes, "I am 40 years old and I never thought I would meet a Westerner, let alone an American. We were taught you were evil and could not have any fun".

And fun we had. Someone had an accordion and one of our members was an excellent player. She began playing polka type music and dancing. A sturdy Russian, very outgoing woman we nicknamed "Mother Russia" took charge, pushed us around to teach us some of their dances. Her black dress with large yellow polka dots, low cut—revealing her amble bosom—was somehow appropriate. Unfortunately, she smelled as if she had not bathed in a month, but it didn't matter, we had such a joyful time.

People are just human the world around and if politics, religion, and ideals wouldn't interfere this would be a much better world. Although we had a severe language barrier, much joy, laughter and good well circulated through the crowd—men dancing with men, men dancing with women, women dancing with women. My inebriated soul was full as someone helped me slush back through the river to the bus—an intercultural experience that I was so fortunate to have and will never forget.

The host chorus in Irkutsk guided us on a trip to another Siberian village with colorfully painted cabins and a wonderful little chapel. A number of their members and ours, including me, stood inside together and began to sing "Salvation is Created"—one of those anthems with a rich, deep sound— in Russian, as we had learned it. I stood with several Russian basses, with that typical, robust Russian sonority and thrilled to blend my voice with theirs. The sounds resonated deep within me and moved me.

We ate lunch at an inn just across a road from Lake Baikal, considered the largest—by volume—and one of the oldest lakes in the world. Its greatest depth is 5,397 ft. Even in the middle of the summer the water temperature is only in the high fifties. One of my friends and I decided to take a very quick dip in this notorious lake, just to say we did. We took turns swimming, just long enough for the other to take a picture. Silly, but a chance not to miss.

That trip, as mentioned above, made me more grateful for our country with all its flaws then I ever had before. It gave me a perspective on the many historical events, including the dictatorship of the Soviet Union, that Germany had invaded Latvia and Estonia, and deep into Russia—that is why German is the second language for many people. I learned that the people are not mean and evil. The human spirit runs deep and survives amidst cruel hardships. I learned, again, that music is truly a universal language, that dance is joyful and unifying.

Spain and Portugal 1994

THE NEXT OVERSEAS TOUR WAS with the Monadnock Chorus to Spain and Portugal. This trip was rather uneventful, in comparison to the cathedral concerts in Italy and the human experiences of New Hampshire Friendship Chorus. But I loved the countries and the people were great. I got used to the daily routine of the Spanish.

    10:00 arise
    10:30 work
    2:00 siesta
    3:00 work
    7:00 tapas
    10:00 dinner
    12:00 party
    3:00 bed.

Our time in Toledo allowed us to fully experience this—and what a beautiful city.

In Seville, another great city, we sang in the beautiful Basilica de la Macarena. The Basilica contains a trove of statues and artwork. It is home to the beautiful statue of the Macarena virgin when it is not on the lead float of the Good Friday parade, the biggest and the most sacred of all the many parades during Holy week. The unique, emotional feature of the Virgin is the five crystal tears flowing down her cheeks.

We embarked on a very scary ferry trip across the Strait of Gibraltar to Tangiers, Morocco. The water was extremely rough, the waves splashing against the windows of the third deck of this huge ship, appropriately the windows of the bar. Morocco was my only visit to a North African culture with its beautiful colors of clothing, rugs, pottery, and art. There were entire streets of noisy hawkers of their goods. That night we were escorted to a typical restaurant with wonderful North African cuisine and serenaded by a local band.

We received our greatest reception in Lisbon, Portugal. It was a rather gloomy day and night, the church was fairly modern and uninspiring, the accompaniment was played on a combination of two electronic keyboards, because none of them had the range of keys that was needed for our pieces. They solved the problem placing them at a 90-degree angle, one having the higher range and one having the lower range. In the practice room an old pump organ served as the keyboard. We had many laughs at our accompanist, George Loring, peddling away.

When the time came for the concert, we were less than enthusiastic, but we soon came alive as the church began to fill with an audience buzzing with eager anticipation. It was still rather chilly and many kept their coats on, but the packed crowd generated a great deal of heat. They were the most appreciative audience of the entire tour. They applauded loudly and verbally exclaimed their enthusiasm. The church provided a small meal, served immediately after the concert. A small, endearing crowd waited for us—about one and a half hours—in the misting rain to waved goodbye until we were out of sight.

Greece 1997

WITH GREAT EXCITEMENT I ANTICIPATED a tour with the Monadnock Chorus, to Greece. Visiting the ancient world of Greece seemed only a pipe dream, but I wanted to explore all the important history those environs would bring. The sights were awe inspiring, where the genesis of our Western civilization began, where there were many discoveries of science, of music theory, where Biblical characters had trod. The daughter of one of our chorus members lived in Athens, so she was able to guide us to some interesting sites there and in small towns away from the big city.

One night as I was conducting a rehearsal, I began to feel more and more intense pain, particularly between my shoulder blades. I finally sat down in a pew and tried to catch my breath. The pains continued and I felt I might be having a heart attack.

The following events became a most interesting insight into another medical world. There was a small medical clinic in town and I was taken there by car. A medical person, I don't remember if she was a doctor, thought I should be transported by what they called an ambulance to an Athens hospital about two hours away. Their version of an ambulance was a small panel truck with a single blue light on top. There was no medical attendant, no medical equipment, not even oxygen, and no bed. I was put on a small stretcher and laid on the floor of the "ambulance". A medical doctor in the chorus traveled with my wife and me to Athens.

The driver raced, through the dark, around the bends and steep hills of the countryside into Athens. I was bounced and jostled about on the floor, trying not to worry. But, I felt that if I were having a heart attack, I couldn't imagine surviving that trip. I surmised we were getting into city as he slowed just a little and I heard more traffic and horns. Suddenly, I heard a bang that sounded like something fell off of the bottom of the truck. My wife told me that we had just sideswiped a parked vehicle, but our driver kept racing toward the hospital.

Oh my, what was to come next was unbelievable! The hospital was a scene of chaos, noise, overcrowding and unclean. The ER was packed with loud, boisterous, people seeking medical attention. No one seemed very ill and I, even though enduring a ride from Hell, was feeling better and not so fearful. I waited along with the rest of the patients.

Our chorus member's daughter arrived, explained my situation, and that I was a famous American conductor. The level of attention spiked immediately and I was examined and directed to check into the hospital for observation.

As I was rolled through the halls, I observed that the hospital was a disaster. Patients lined the halls sitting in chairs, wheelchairs and lying on gurneys. I was rolled into a crowded room with three other people, one on the verge of death. She was revived once, but soon succumbed with a strong death rattle. The entire hospital was dirty and had only a hint of being sanitized. The restroom was across the hall with bugs climbing the walls and cockroaches scurrying across the floor into the corners. The meals, during my stay, were of cold, overcooked chicken breast, some tepid vegetables, tea and bread.

However, I got wonderful treatment from a team of doctors, who were very concerned about this "famous" American conductor. Each morning they came in as a team, usually four, and discussed my prognosis. Most of them were trained in England or the U.S. and spoke quite good English.

They prescribed an angiogram, to determine whether an artery was blocked. I was skeptical, to say the least, but there were not many rational options. The procedure went smoothly, and they said that only one artery was blocked about 40 per cent, but shouldn't have given me problems.

A godsend was a wonderful Greek man, in the adjacent bed who palliated my stay in the hospital. Bill had been a staff member of the Greek attaché and his English was good. We talked and talked about life in the U.S., Greek life and culture, politics, family and we became good friends by the time I departed. I met his wife and daughter, who was a fair pianist by his account. They didn't speak English, but Bill translated a lot.

Bill had some knowledge of classical music and was fascinated to meet a conductor. I assured him I was not famous, but was privileged to be living a life full of musical experiences I couldn't have dreamed of as a child. We kept in touch for quite a few years, sending letters and gifts, until he had some more heart problems and the letters stopped. What a blessing he was!

After three long days, the doctors approved my leaving the hospital and gave me permission to fly on our scheduled flight home in two days.

At our usual departure party, the night before we left, I was a hit with my "Top ten reasons not to go to a Greek hospital" a la David Letterman.

South Africa 1998

A TOUR OF AFRICA LEFT some deep impressions on me in every way. The board of the New Hampshire Friendship Chorus invited me to conduct them on a tour to South Africa, another opportunity I could only have dreamed of. Ever since my Uncle James and family spent 10 years in Tanganyika as missionaries, came home with amazing stories, pictures and souvenirs, I thought of going to Africa. Books like, *Cry, my beloved Country,* movies like *Out of Africa* only heightened that desire.

Given the NHFC's mission, we shared concerts with a number of different, local choirs with amazing connections and interactions. I had told our African tour director that I wanted to see all variety of cultures living in South Africa, not just the lily-white population. He obliged and provided us with a wonderful cross section of the country.

The black South African people are gorgeous humans beings, men and women—tall, very dark skinned without a blemish, from the humidity, I guess. They are joyful, happy people—music, instruments, singing and dance are a huge part of their culture. I was fortunate to experience much of this culture.

Our first concert was shared with the famed Paarl children's choir. It was first formed in 1984 with underprivileged children. In 1985 the first home to house them was built. Now there are a number of homes and a number of choirs. Their motto is: "Helping Africa's most vulnerable children today, so they can help Africa tomorrow!" What beautiful children and how well they sang.

In Cape Town, our bus was greeted by a New Orleans style band, formed by a group of "colored" men, dressed in bright costumes and in white face. "Colored" is not a dirty word in South Africa. It is a designation for anyone who isn't black or white. They usually have a mixture of bloodlines. What a hoot! It must have been quite a sight as they led us in a procession from the bus to the hall. A nice meal was provided and they performed a jazzy type concert for us, and we sang a couple of our lighter numbers, but it was their show. I still have the brightly colored, sparkly, minstrel-like jacket that the director, respectfully, bestowed on me.

The next evening, we performed with a Zulu choir that performed somewhat classical music at the beginning of their program, but with each segment they moved the clock back in history and performed music with costumes and traditional dances from earlier times.

By the end of the concert, the men wore only small sheepskins around their loins, carried weapons of all kinds including the mace, swords and bows and yelled their scary war cries. The women wore a variety of dress, often with see through blouses with no bras, skirts, and bra tops like a bikini top or topless. All were barefoot.

Our concert was in a non-descript concert hall, with a large stage that could easily accommodate the combined choirs of some 150 members. When the formal concert ended, we moved onto the stage together and danced until the hall needed to be closed. We knew a couple of African songs and they taught us a number, by rote. This old nimble of foot, was still young enough to keep up with them.

The concert in the Regina Mundi church, located in Soweto, provided the setting for another life highlight. This church became notorious as a sanctuary for many black Africans during the persecution by the apartheid. Mandela was arrested in this church and the young moderator of the concert said the last time he had been in that church, he was in hiding.

A multi tribal chorus met us with great grace and spirit. We were the first large group of Americans—some 90 of us—to come to that church since the break up of the apartheid. About 1000 people packed the church, many in their historical tribal dress. The clothing was worn in many layers of very bright colors, particularly yellows and blues. Men and women wore similar clothing—a flowing dress, robe like garb, with colorful hats. With the proper knowledge, one could identify the tribe by their dress. We were told that these people, although they had come to Soweto to find jobs, were still strongly attached to their original tribes.

We sang a short part of our program first and then their choir sang. They began the program with more contemporary choral music from African composers. They ended with traditional music from the various tribes, with many members of those tribes in the choir and in the audience. When a song representing a certain tribe was sung, the people in the audience of that tribe would stand up, yell, clap, wave their arms, while dancing in the aisles with great spirit.

I was sitting in the front row wondering how we could tap into that enthusiasm—I didn't want our second time on stage to detract from that. In research for this trip, I had bought a book of South African Freedom Songs. I randomly picked a song, "Halleluya! Pelo Tsa Roma", from the book, mainly for its upbeat feeling—a simple praise song. So, I thought, we would start off with this song.

Our choir moved on to the stage and we began to sing this song. Wow, the audience exploded behind me—I wasn't sure what was going on, but took a peak over my shoulder. The audience was loudly cheering, clapping, weeping, hugging each other in a reaction that I have never experience before or since. I had chosen the song that was their signature "Freedom Song". It was as special to them as our "We shall Overcome" during the Civil Rights movement. The fact that a bunch of white folks would sing it in an African church, that special Soweto church, evoked a load of passion. We sang a few more of our lighter numbers and ended the program. Their choir came on stage and intermingled with ours and we repeated that song several times. Our chorus members reported, afterward of holding hands, of hugging, of tears shed with the Africans beside them.

The director wanted to give me a gift, and offered either their drum, which was hewn out of a log with cow skin for a top or his mace that he had warlike brandished around the stage. I took the drum and it is a sacred piece for me today.

A mystical event of the human spirit happened that night. To me, there was a god, a creator, a spirit that moved in that hall—again displaying love, friendship, humanity, joy and peace.

To add icing to the cake we went to a small tavern nearby, which was supposedly closed for our party/reception. But a few curious Africans remained as we entered. Drinks were distributed and I think there was food, but so unimportant that I don't remember what it was.

A small band began to play and people started to dance. The few Africans who hadn't left joined in. Again, our members were moved and inspired by the comments of the natives, that this had never happened before—white people in that lowly tavern. I stood beside a local man, in the bathroom, who expressed his deep gratitude for our coming there. It didn't seem to me anything unusual, but then, I hadn't lived under the segregation and demeaning oppression of the apartheid for many years as he had.

We were, also, given a tour of the really poor Soweto. We saw the cardboard city, literally, small structures built out of cardboard and any kind of protective material—rows and rows of these structures.

Other tours included a visit to Mandela's former home, a brandy distillery—tasting a truly great brandy. We took a safari in the Kruger National Park seeing four of the big five, only missing the leopard. We slept at a motel at the edge of the park and golfed the next day with a required caddy—signs on the course read, "Don't try to retrieve your ball from the water, there are crocodiles and hippos".

We enjoyed an early evening safari, in a land rover into the woods and saw the southern white rhino up close. That evening, a trip up a hill in a large jeep-like vehicle provided sunsets of spectacular beauty and views across the hills and valleys. We could hear the drums of the evening ritual—our guide told us—many miles across the valley, an eerie sound that jarred one's imagination of the activities involved.

We visited a replica of a Zulu village, a production for tourists by a theatrical group that dramatically performed many of the old Zulu dances, in costumes—topless men and women, a witch doctor with a huge bosom, missing a lot of teeth and braless, men pounding warring drums and making warlike maneuvers. There were grass-roofed huts appointed with handcrafted furniture and cooking pots hanging over small fires.

Another awesome ride on the motorcycle.

Carnegie Hall 1998

I NEVER DREAMED I WOULD have an opportunity to conduct in one of the most famed performing spaces in the world. Remember as a kid, I couldn't dream of it, because I didn't know of it.

I mentioned that as I was settling into my position at Keene State, I met Peter Tiboris who was settling into his position at our sister College, Plymouth State College. We somehow got in touch with each other and started a long time friendship. In the early eighties, I discovered that after Peter departed Plymouth State and another teaching position, he had started an organization called, MidAmerica Productions—an organization that invited choirs across the country to form a mass choir which performed some huge choral/orchestral work in Avery Fisher Hall in Lincoln Center

I signed up my Chamber Singers at KSC in 1982. Many of my students had never ventured out of New Hampshire and had never visited New York City. They sang with group of about 400 singers of all ages and locations. They performed three *Te Deums*, one by Berlioz, Bruckner and Walton. The Berlioz is seldom performed because it requires massive forces to produce. It was spectacular, with ensembles stationed all over the hall providing a cacophony of sound that was thrilling. The students, I'm sure, will never forget it.

I kept in touch with Peter over the years and as the quality of the Mondnack Chorus performances grew, I would send him some recordings. He sometimes would write me a kind, appreciated, review. In January of 1998, I received a call from Peter who said, "I have an opening on a program in Carnegie Hall, on April 26 for about 45 minutes. Would you bring the Monadnock Chorus"? I was flabbergasted and immediately said, "Of course"! There were hurdles to jump—board's approval, logistics of all kinds and performing at a level worthy of Carnegie Hall.

The board was very enthusiastic, the wheels started turning to solve the logistics and we began rehearsing in earnest. When the word got out that we were going to Carnegie Hall, the membership swelled from about 100 singers to about 140 singers.

I had already chosen the repertoire for our Peterborough concert and decided to pick the best from that to sing in the famed hall. A number of the works were to be accompanied by a brass quartet, so I decided to perform those and a commissioned work by New York composer, David Earnest. This would be the New York debut of his work.

We excitedly loaded into a number of buses, and headed to NYC for a short afternoon rehearsal in the Hall, before the concert. As we drove by the front of the Hall, there was my photo on the side of the marque with other much more famous performers. What a rush!

As I began the rehearsal, we needed some stands and chairs moved and a couple chorus members came to adjust them. The union guys quickly came forth and curtly informed us we weren't allowed to do. They were contracted to do it and we couldn't lift a hand.

There were other incidents that made me aware that the professional life at that level was different. Between the rehearsal and the concert we had to change into concert dress—tuxedos—and I was going toward the dressing areas where chorus men were changing, when a staff member of the Hall came by and said; "Ah no, Maestro, you need to use the conductor's room" and led me to an upper, private room with pictures of likes of Brahms, Bernstein and Mahler hanging on the walls.

The performance itself was very heady and humbling at the same time. The acoustics, of course, makes one sound better than you are. Standing on the podium where all the great conductors stood, overwhelmed me at times. The chorus members laughed at me after the concert and said my bow over the podium railing was long and slow. I said, of course—I knew I would probably never stand there again and looking into that great hall with all its balconies was daunting and I wanted it etched in my memory, as it is.

When I gave the last cut-off to the music, I hustled off stage and a person was standing there with a bottle of Perrier and a soft white towel to wipe the sweat. I said I could get used to that kind of treatment and jokingly told my chorus members I expected that treatment from now on.

The irony of "shit on my boots to Carnegie Hall" was not lost amidst all the emotions of that day. How blessed and fortunate I was to have experienced that great moment from my humble beginnings. That day is forever tucked away in my psychic, soul and spirit to be brought out periodically to enjoy.

Scandinavia 2000

AFTER THAT UNFORGETTABLE HIGH, MY life and career continued. My last tour with the Monadnock Chorus took us to the beautiful countries of Norway, Sweden and Denmark. In addition to the music, the views—the land with its rolling hills were exquisite, the magnificent ocean shores and fjords, the beautiful old cities, and the wonderful people.

It was interesting to observe and question the culture and politics of those very neutral countries. Historically, they are some of the most peaceful countries in the world. There were a lot of stories and monuments to their aiding in the escape of many Jews during WW II. Many of the churches in Denmark were used as a refuge for those Jews.

Some chorus members were curious about the Socialist government and how it worked. Our guide was queried about the amount of taxes the citizens pay—about 50 per cent. The guide spoke with great pride, "But we are covered from birth to grave. We have free education to a doctorate, if we desire; I have three children, all born in wonderful hospitals free, I just entered my mother into a lovely retirement home on the government's tab".

I started to wonder how much I pay in taxes of some kind and how little I receive in return, besides a huge military—our infrastructure is in terrible condition, huge medical insurance costs, education expenses skyrocketing. What is wrong here?

A most memorable stay was in the small town of Vadstena. We stayed in the Vadstena Klosterhotel, the surviving buildings of an ancient monastery where the smells and aura of the original remained. The stonewalls were cool, but the rooms cozy. Vadstena is situated on the beautiful Lake Vättern, Sweden's second largest *lake. We sang in the old chapel of the monastery* and had a wonderful audience that filled the old chapel and responded with great enthusiasm to our performance.

In Denmark, the American ambassador, who was from New Hamphire, hosted us for a short concert by the pool and a lot of good food. Another time, we serenaded a group of Swedes in a public park. As we sang, a crowd gathered and we mingled with the people—tall, blond, beautiful people.

Jonathan Daniels
Concert 2005

KEENE NATIVE JONATHAN DANIELS, A seminarian who graduated from the Navel Academy in Virginia, went to the south to become involved in the Civil Rights movement. He was killed in 1965, shielding an African-American girl from a bullet fired by an angry storeowner, who was upset by a group of white and black civil rights workers wanting to enter his store.

Daniels remains a hero of that movement and continues to be honored in Keene and across the country. In 2005, the 40th year of his death, the city developed a weeklong celebration of his life. A cantata, which had been commissioned a year earlier, and premiered at the Navel Academy, became the center of a service of remembrances and tributes to Daniels.

I was invited to conduct this cantata, *A Journey to Freedom, Honor and Glory*, composed by Julius Williams. I recruited many singers from area choruses, including the Monadnock Chorus, hired wonderful soloists and an excellent professional orchestra. The lyrics are powerful and the music varied—a mixture of classical, jazz and spirituals style fits the lyrics perfectly.

The woman whose life Daniels saved spoke, old childhood friends and neighbors shared their memories. An African-American friend of mine moderated the program with great grace and style. The entire evening evoked another emotional, spiritual and musical moment for me—a place where my Mennonite heritage of pacifism, concern for our fellow humans, and music merged into one great experience. I had Mennonite friends who went south to become involved, like Daniels. I really wanted to go, but again, it was too risky for my family and maybe for me too at the time. I must say, for quite a while, I felt guilty.

China 2005, China and Tibet 2006

AN INVITATION CAME AGAIN TO conduct the New Hampshire Friendship Chorus on a foreign tour and provided me two opportunities to visit China.

The tour agency, the board tour director and I went there the summer of 2005 to scope out some of our hotels, concert venues, and restaurants. We didn't visit all the places in the interior of China, but spent time in some of the biggest cities where the choir would perform—Shanghai and Beijing.

The unusual human experience of this trip was an evening in the bar of one of the hotels in Beijing. Some of our group was going to explore the city's nightlife. Tired as I was, I decided to stay at the hotel, go to the bar for a couple drinks and go to bed early. The bar was quite empty except for the bar tender and a couple young ladies sitting on the stools. I went to the other side of the bar and ordered a drink. They all spoke very little English so the communication was a mixture of words and gestures, not too clear.

Soon the young ladies moved over and sat on either side of me and the light bulb lit up—Duh! Soon gestures, touches made me very aware what was up. I tried to explain to them that I was not interested in their services. One departed and the other cozied up and we conversed in short sentences and expressions.

Thank god, another woman entered and I realized quickly that she was American. She sat beside me and we had a fun conversation. She was in the city for a number of months on some business venture and was starving for some English conversation. She had been at this bar before and noted that there was Karaoke, when she discovered that I was a singer.

The plea went up for me to sing. I don't like Karaoke and declined. The "lady of the night" got up and sang in a horrible voice and way out of tune— the American lady sang next with a better rendition. I guess I had just enough to drink by that time to get up the courage to sing. I sang "Old Man River" in a bass key that suited me well.

My fans were very pleased, amused and impressed. I may have sung another one, but don't remember what it was. I headed off to an early sleep and the young girl dogged me down the hall with my continued explanation, it wasn't going to happen. Finally she left me.

The next summer—2006, the choir departed for its tour. It was another dream I couldn't have had as a young Mennonite farm boy. The only thing I knew about China were expressions such as: " digging all the way down to China" or when not wanting to eat something, my mother would say: "I bet there are a lot of hungry kids in China who would love to have that".

We left from Boston, flew to San Francisco and to Beijing. The eleven-hour flight to China was overnight and even at the age of 66 it was very taxing—do I sit and try to sleep or do I get up every hour or so to keep from generating blood clots?

Beijing is a very old, beautiful, historical city, filled with museums of art and artifacts. We sang with a choir in a beautiful concert hall. I was single again for this trip and the beautiful Asian women choir members enjoyed having pictures taken with me. I didn't mind. Who doesn't like being a celebrity?

China provided another unimaginable glimpse into to very ancient history, as well as some modern events. An eerie feeling set in my stomach as we walked the cobblestones of Tiananmen Square, remembering the revolt there in 1989 and the much displayed image of the little Chinese guy standing bravely in front of a huge tank. Looking into the Forbidden City and the stories of the emperor and his dowagers—concubines, I pictured what the life was like in that ancient culture.

The Great Wall, another one of the great wonders of the world I was privileged to visit, is indeed an awesome sight. As I walked along it, I imagined the thousands of Chinese laborers, with crude equipment who constructed this massive structure. As I peered out from the towers, over the countryside, I could visualize the fierce battles that took place there.

A flight into the interior of China brought many new sights and events. Our guide, who was born and raised in China, until she immigrated to Canada some years ago, had arranged for us to visit a small village out in the boonies where, until ten years ago, the people were living in caves. Now, small concrete block huts were erected for them by a gravel company, for which they toiled. We toured their former homes, the caves, now open for view. Only a few artifacts, furniture and a cot remained.

Although having some more modern equipment, much of the gravel work was still done by hand—literally breaking large rocks into small ones. The villagers, young and old, children and grandparents lined the road as we wandered into the village.

The mayor held a reception with a meal for us. The menu included some raw delicacies, some that didn't look too appetizing—I usually try the cuisine of any country I visit—but not this time. It was amazing that they could provide food, at all, after I saw the tiny kitchen with very crude stoves. But to have a stove at all, meant that this family was well off.

The mayor's "mansion" was filled with what was probably quite expensive and artsy appointments and reflected their status in the community. There would be worse in Tibet, but to that point, the outside toilet was absolutely the worst—extremely smelly in the hot temperature. There were just a couple holes in the ground over which you squatted and hoped for the best.

We traveled to visit the "terracotta soldiers", located just outside the city of Xi'; their history insightful. In all my travels, nothing competed with this view of the after life. An emperor thought he needed an army to protect him in the after life. He had these soldiers, horses and carriages carved. It took 700,000 men working 30 years to build this army of soldiers sculpted out of terra cotta, lined up in row after row—archeologists estimate about 8000 figures. They were buried in a structure under the ground for preservation and protection. The work was halted in 209 BC. The next emperor discovered them and for fear that this army would defeat him after he died, had the structure burnt down and the soldiers covered with dirt.

In 1974, a farmer, digging a well, uncovered a terra cotta head. Fortunately, he didn't just toss it aside, but took it to a minister of culture. After study, the minister's hypothesis was that it was a part of this long lost army. As excavation began he obviously was correct. The digging revealed the broken, dismembered soldiers. Bit by bit many have been reconstructed and placed back in rows. There are many hundreds finished and displayed, but they aren't even finished digging.

It's quite a sight as you look over rows of soldiers, each face different, believed to ape the face of the sculptor, various insignias and uniforms, indicating the different level of officers. Chariots with six horse teams lead some of the rows of soldiers. After the finished rows, one can see how the parts of bodies lay randomly on the ground by their destruction. An area where the parts were being reassembled was called the "hospital".

This is, truly, an unbelievable view into the minds of a culture, with a deep mixture of spiritual beliefs and politics and the after life—in a completely different way than the Judeo-Christian culture of the U.S. We visited numerous religious sites and temples with great fascination. Another opportunity to see religious/spiritual views far distant from my upbringing.

From there we took a long, eight-hour train ride to Shanghai. Hundreds of stinky Chinese crowded into this double decker train. Quickly the toilets piled up with sewage as you can imagine. Hot temperatures, in the nineties, exacerbated the problem. The trip did give us a view of the rural landscape with its crude farming, people still living in caves—the poor of the poor. I saw members of a family I guessed, men, women and children hand harvesting crops of hay, corn and other vegetables, on the side of the hills—so steep I don't know how they kept their balance.

As we approached Shanghai, one began to see the huge development of that city. The suburbs teemed with construction of high-rise apartment buildings, the techniques and machinery still appearing very out dated, by our standards. However, downtown Shanghai exhibits some of the best of the Chinese economy, displayed in huge modern architectural skyscrapers that flood the horizon, beautifully lit up at night. The structures were truly works of art, whether you liked them or not, designed by some of the greatest building architects in the world.

The hustle and bustle of both Beijing and Shanghai included people of all walks of life on vehicles as varied as bicycles, motor scooters with women dressed to the nines—I assumed going to an office--rickshaws, farmers with small tractors pulling carts carrying their goods, smoking busses, all trying to find their path in a street without any lanes. I don't know how the driver of our big bus negotiated through that entanglement without running over someone.

In the morning it was amusing to look out my hotel window, to the public square below, and see people practicing tai chi and other eastern forms of exercise.

As an option at the end of our formal choir tour, we could take several side trips. I chose the one to Tibet, for I knew that I likely would never get that close again and as I aged I wouldn't be able to tolerate the high altitude.

We departed from Chengdu, and the view from the plane exposed unbelievable views of the mountains and valleys, the tiny villages nestled in those valleys, making me wonder of the activities, the lives of the villagers.

We got off the plane, in Lhasa at 10,000 ft. Immediately, I felt the effects of the high altitude. I never was incapacitated with altitude sickness, but I suffered a great deal with shortness of breath, headaches and some dizziness. My room was on the second floor, with only about seven steps to a landing, and seven more. I could only negotiate a couple steps and then had to catch my breath.

Our guide swore by a tea that we all had to drink and it may have kept me from going over the edge, but I am so glad I took the opportunity to visit another culture so different than anything I had experienced before.

It is the land of Buddhism, the Dalai Lama, prayer wheels, strict times of prayer every day, colorful garments, sandaled feet, and scrumptious food. The tour included a visit to the 13 story-high Potala Palace—the Palace where the 5th Dalai Lama is entombed. It is still inhabited today by a few Buddhist monks and was the current Dalai Lama's home before he left the country for India during the 1959 Tibetan uprising. The hundreds of steps up to the open parts of the palace presented a challenge, but I figured that if I couldn't make it, I would stop and come back down. I really wanted to see the inside of this beautiful palace and witness its religious significance. I took my time, rested frequently and made it. The reward for my efforts was the decorative rooms that sparkled with bright gold figures, the Buddha sculptures, the magnificent tomb of the 5th Dalai Lama and many other religious artifacts

One day we took a trip to the Sera Monastery. Each week the monks gathered in the yard around the Monastery to perform a intentional, very public ritual—passionate, religious debates, yelling arguments with each other. One had to wonder if it wasn't more about the theater than about the transference of dogma. An aside! A distinctive memory of this place was the worst toilets that I have experienced in all my travel.

Cultures like this, leave me wondering about our often myopic view of the before and the after life of our current existence on this earth, our Western, Judeo-Christian view of the world, our religious dogma. I was taught, of course, that our culture and history is the "only" way to live—to experience salvation and go to Heaven. Jesus said, "I am the Way, the Truth, and the Light, no one comes to Father, but by me" (John 14:6). I heard many times that people in these cultures were doomed to Hell, and we had a responsibility to bring them the "Gospel" so that they had the same chance we had of meriting heaven and that the statues of Buddhas were "graven images—idols, and the living ones were "false gods". The idea of coming back, after death, in any form was scoffed at.

The goal of Heaven, the avoidance of Hell, was a huge part of our Faith. Mom's favorite sayings, prayers, gospel songs spoke of the sweetness of the reward of walking on "streets of gold", "sitting at the feet of Jesus", "never having pain and sorrow", "meeting Peter at the Gates of Heaven" meeting with loved ones gone before. These weren't metaphors to evangelical and fundamentalist believers like us. These, we believed, were reality.

I still choose the Christian way of life, because I believe it is a good way to live, not a path to the "Pearly Gates of Heaven. I choose it by "faith" not by proof. But over my lifetime, having been exposed to many other beliefs, I cannot assume that the belief of my heritage is the only one.

The three trips with the New Hampshire Friendship Chorus provided some of the greatest highlights of my life. I will never forget the amazing feeling of Soweto, the fun and human connections of the dancing in a cow pie strewn pasture in the middle of Siberia, the celebration of July 4th in Riga, witnessing the religious culture of Tibet, the Great Wall and many more.

Retirement from the Monadnock Chorus 2009

～ᴇ

As I ᴀᴘᴘʀᴏᴀᴄʜᴇᴅ ᴛʜᴇ ᴀɢᴇ of 70, I began to think of my aging and how my life, personal and professional would/could change. I began to think of retirement from the Monadnock Chorus and from the college.

As my 20 years of tenure with the Chorus neared, a goal that I set for myself, I began to think of my achievements and that it was time to walk away. I had fulfilled many musical goals with them. I had the opportunity to travel, to grow as a musician and to conduct a lot of great works on my bucket list. I increased the quality of the performances to acclaim by audiences and press. I was involved with a wonderful group of people.

Times were changing and I didn't necessarily view it as a good change. A lot of the old guard, singers and board members, had served their time and had eased up or had passed away. Younger people with different ideas became active, and political agendas were debated leading sometimes to splits within the board and in ideas of the future.

Performing the great choral works with professional orchestras and soloists inspired me deeply, fulfilling the dreams I had in graduate school, where I experienced these type of works for the first time. Raising money was becoming more difficult with the down economy. I surmised that this would change the whole repertoire of the chorus, having to perform pieces with smaller instrumental ensembles or just piano, selecting more modern popular works.

So, I announced my retirement in 2008. Choosing the last work was an easy task—the Verdi *Requiem* one more time. I had wonderful soloists and a truly fine orchestra. Many of the chorus members had sung it before and I invited students from the college to join us. The blend of younger and older voices made the choral sound spectacular. The performance reached the level deserving of my last performance. Emotions ran high in my head as I wielded the baton, directing them for the last time.

A new director, who played in the orchestra, had been chosen and after the last cut off, and after extended, enthusiastic applause, I called him to the front of the stage and literally passed my baton to him, as a few tears were shed by him and me, and some in the audience.

When most of the audience had left, the chair of the board called me to the front of the Town House and most of the chorus gathered around. She had something to give me. I was unaware that the chorus was informed that a box was placed on the registration table for several rehearsals for them to deposit money for my gifts. I opened the box and there lay a beautiful watch—I learned later, a Movado—a very expensive watch. I could only exclaim "Holy Crap". And it went on—a great bottle of champagne and a wad of cash, I believe $400. I half jokingly have said, "Either they really wanted to get rid of me or they really liked me".

Humility, pride, satisfaction, and fulfillment rushed to my spirit and soul. The run was unbelievable and I am so grateful for the privilege to work with wonderful people and musicians—the privilege to conduct some of the greatest of music literature. I will forever be thankful and feel blessed by that rewarded endeavor.

Final years at Keene State College 2009 - 2015

THE BEST THING ABOUT MY teaching career were the students, the worst thing was the politics of academia and the department. I would have left KSC many years ago, but I had the position I really wanted, teaching in both the vocal and choral areas. I loved the combination of teaching voice and conducting choirs. With all the bullshit, I had my little kingdom and could demand my standards. When I talked to my colleagues at bigger, better institutions, they had the same complaints about the politics of the music department, but didn't have the independence that I had.

Throughout the years, I demanded high standards and in my younger days, as I would say "when I was full of piss and vinegar", I sometimes got so frustrated at a poor rehearsal; I lost my temper and stomped out of the room. It generally got their attention and they shaped up. One of the first times it happened, I closed my music, and told them rehearsal was over and we wouldn't hold another one until they were ready to be serious. I told them that music was a sacred thing to me and they shouldn't f * k up my profession, departed to my office, which was attached to the rehearsal room, and closed the door.

I could hear that the students just set there for a while I think stunned, then began talking, but I couldn't hear what they were saying and then there was a knock at my door. My best three students were sent to check on me.

They wondered if I was O.K. I had simmered down by that time, and I said I was fine, but meant every word I said.

These standards and honesty sometimes got me in trouble. I strived, through the years, to be honest with students about their potential and their progress. Some students channeled it into more dedication, more attention to details and to practice more. Others took it as an insult, ran to mommy and the mommy called the Dean to complain that I was too harsh and that I destroyed all their hopes and dreams. Teaching for 40+ years at the college, I could see a trend toward more and more of these events.

Many students were becoming a product of leniency from parents and the educational institutions. They were led to believe that they could achieve anything to which they aspired. And yes, people can achieve anything up to a certain point. But we all have various degrees of talent or skill in certain fields. Talent in music is endowed. Levels of musical ability range from none to geniuses. There is a level of ability below which you can't perform as a musician. We are in a period of what I call "self esteem run amok". So, when someone like me said, "I'm sorry, but you just weren't given enough talent to rise to the level of competency in music: it was natural for them to feel insulted. I always felt that sooner or later, someone had to tell them and sooner is better. Students have not been taught respect and the value of advice from people with far more experience and education than they have.

In the last number of years, more and more students expected that just because they liked music and started a program that nothing should interfere, not performance level, not ability nor accomplishments. They thought that if they strived to become better that they should be rewarded. Unfortunately, that is not always the case. I believe that you don't get an A just for effort, but are also bound by that inherent gift.

I would often relate this story. I am 5 foot 7 inches, had limited athletic ability and, even with tremendous dedication, desire and hard work, could never have been a professional basketball player. I knew, long time ago, that I did not have the talent to be a visual artist. Not everyone can be a successful musician—as I would tell students you are limited by your ability to hear pitches, to sing in tune, and/or have an adequate voice.

In the last five years of my full-time teaching, I was called into the Dean's office two times, for consultations about some complaints from two students. One student was an advisee, a performance major, who had a pretty voice, but was never going to meet the standards of the competitive world out there. This student also could not pass theory and had to take parts of it multiple times. My advice to the student was to seek some other profession in which he/she was more talented and perform music with a local band at different venues. The student was very offended and ran to mommy who called the Dean.

Another student had problems in the pre-recital jury and I was blunt in my judgment. The result was as above, a call to the Dean's office. As I mentioned, I felt an obligation to be honest with a students about their ability.

Sometimes that kick in the pants gave the underachiever a boost to practice more, to listen to the advice of their professors and make great strides. As an example, during these trying times with the Dean, I had a student, Nicole, that I called in and advised that she was not going to make it as a performance major. As always, I said I would be glad to be proven wrong. Well, she set her jaw and proved me wrong. She gave very accomplished junior and senior recitals. I told her numerous times how proud I am of her. So as the general student requirements were becoming less stringent and many students were getting degrees that really weren't valid, it seemed a good time to retire.

In those last years, I was privileged to teach mostly wonderful students who went on to fine graduate schools and conservatories, or to teaching and/ or performance careers. I maintained a voice studio of a number of really fine students—talented, motivated and respectful. When you teach music, and particularly music with words—art songs, choral music, and opera composed on great poetry or stories—one has the opportunity to share ideas, philosophies, culture, and style as you try to teach good performance. The voice is so connected to the body, mind and soul that study thereof is very personal. Your real life experiences—love, anger, disappointment, illness, and failure all affect your voice. So a voice teacher often becomes a parent, confessor, mentor, and psychologist to his students. They became family to my wife, Marcia, and me who they adore. Several of my students began to call me

"Babbo"—father in Italian, a term very familiar to singers, sung in the great aria from *Gianni Schicchi*, "O mio babbino caro". Many of my students, from all my years of teaching, keep in touch particularly through the social media

When I decided to retire, I didn't take on any new students, but had five yet to graduate. I wanted to continue teaching them and they wanted to continue to study with me—it can be traumatic to change voice teachers in midstream. Those remaining very talented students were a joy to teach. With great pride I watched three become accepted into the New England Conservatory, and other excellent institutions like Boston Conservatory, Boston University, Peabody and UMass/Amherst.

With conflicting emotions, I retired—having given a lot of energy, commitment, and dedication to Keene State College, the Music Department, the music program and thousands of students for 35 years. KSC provided for me a stage from which I continued to develop as a teacher, conductor and voice teacher. My Oratorio Society had a great run and gave me many satisfying experiences with some amazing acclaim both from the press and the audience. Financially, I earned a decent living and the college funded trips to great conventions and workshops, like the Oregon Bach Festival, and three wonderful sabbaticals.

But, it was a good time to retire from KSC Music Department as the face of the department and the goals of the program changed, with new faculty members' input, the dynamics of the politics changed.

Coda

AFTER MY SECOND DIVORCE, I declared to anyone who would listen, but particularly friends and relatives, "I am never getting married again". A number of them replied, "You'd better not, or we'll kick your butt". I bought a house on Pearly Pond in Rindge, NH—my dream of living on a lake—and settled into a single life.

My friends and neighbors filled the void of a spouse and I was, somewhat content. But, I am not an anti-social being; I thrive on an intimate relationship of many levels. Missing this in the single life, I joined "Match.com"—I never was good at picking up woman in a bar or elsewhere. Pickup lines were not my forte and I shied away in fear of being misunderstood or rejected. I dated a few women, one for an extended time, but nothing seemed plausible—better alone than another failed marriage.

In my tenure with the Monadnock Chorus, numerous people, men, women and couples became my friends, at various levels of closeness. Marcia was one of those choristers—she grew up in York, PA, 40 miles from my home—who became a friend, partly for that demographic connection. She recognized my weird Chambersburg accent at my first rehearsal with MC.

We never met outside of the rehearsal; she never toured with us, but just always a friendly smile and little hugs. I, of course, didn't know she was in a troubled marriage and she was unaware that my marriage was decaying. After we both moved out of our marriages, we began to see each other and fell deeply in love.

Marcia is, the overused phrase, my soul mate. The question is: Why didn't fate bring us together sooner? Marcia's joyful, quirky, funny, positive personality fulfills much of which I "ain't", at least no one drew this out of me before now.

As I am finishing this memoir in 2016, I am only at the beginning of my full time retirement. The relief I feel from the stressful logistics of working is tempered by the sadness of not making music. Making music lifts my spirits, fills my heart, and edifies my soul. Music replaced formal religion, often providing much more connection to the "Holy Other" than church services. I do miss the experience of my performances that I shared with fellow talented musicians and the audiences. I fed on the privilege of lifting their spirits, often bringing tears to their eyes from various emotions evoked. Devoid of this, I am left feeling a bit bereft at times. It will remain to be seen how I can fill that void.

The summer of 2010, one of Marcia's cousins and wife came for a visit. I hadn't met them, but I saw on Facebook that they owned a big cabin cruiser on Tom's River in New Jersey. I told Marcia that I hoped I liked them and they me, because I'd like an invitation to go out on that boat. We did have a wonderful time and I floated the idea of a trip on their boat. They replied that they were selling it.

It is an older boat, but in good condition and immediately I thought of buying it, and made a trip down to NJ to see it. After Washington and my boat experience there, every time I would visit a place with a marina of boats, I'd walk among them and drool. It is a 36 ft Carver—one of the best brands—with dual 250 horse motors, sleeps four, has a flying bridge where the boat is piloted.

I had it trucked to Lake Champlain to a marina in Charlotte, Vermont, a few miles from Burlington. I have always loved Burlington—Scott lived there for several years—and I visited him and wandered down to the piers and dreamed of owning one of those big boats.

That boat offered me fulfillment of another item on my bucket list and a dream. It provided church for me on many occasions. We spent many wonderful weekends on that boat, sometimes just enjoying sleeping on it and visiting some of the sights of the area, such as the Shelburne Museum with a fabulous historical collection of many items, the Shelburne Farm, Charlotte country store and the Saturday Farmers' Market.

We plied the great Lake Chaplain—the sixth largest in the country—and were mesmerized by many glorious sunsets while sitting on the bridge with our wine or cocktail. We celebrated our granddaughter's fifth birthday out on the water. From the bridge of our docked boat, we had a wonderful view of the Green Mountains of Vermont to the east and a view of the Adirondacks of New York to the west. We enjoyed many breath takingly, beautiful sunsets, with drink in hand, music playing and listening to the clanging of the sailboats' rigging.

But it is time to sell it. The saying that "a boat is just a hole in the water where you throw your money" is fortuitous. But, the experience was priceless.

I am so fortunate and blessed to end up in this wonderful house on Pearly Pond. The lake provides many opportunities of worship for me. I often sit on our upper deck, with great attention and enjoyment, listening to all the birds' songs, watching the birds winging to the feeder only a few feet away, for their morning feed. The nuthatches, chickadees, gold, house and purple finches, tufted titmice, the hummingbirds, the grackles—bully nuisances— with a quick diverted route after catching a glance of me sitting there. I hear the cardinal in the tree nearby singing his glorious songs. Pesky chipmunks scurry around on the patio below, stuffing into their cheeks with pieces of the moldy bread that I dropped from the deck, the gray squirrels speedily chasing each other through the trees. We have beavers swimming by, sometimes otters frolicking in the water close by, a mink dashing across our little beach. This year, 2016, many varieties of diving, migrating ducks have returned after a few years of not stopping by: mergansers, scaups, buffleheads and once in a while a lone loon.

Today, I experience the Holy Other's presence in many different ways. My spiritual reality has moved from the church building and religious institutions, to many other situations. For example, after listening to a recording of the great tenor, Luciano Pavorotti, on the way to the golf course, I called to a very good, musician friend to come to my car, that I had just been to church.

Sometimes sitting on the deck for a while and enjoying the nature around, Marcia enters and I say; "Sssh, I'm in church".

My spiritual life has settled into a rhythm of many things—seeing the Holy Other in fellow beings, in nature and in some unexplained events. I mentioned the whip-poor-will appearance after Daddy died. From my first visit to Marcia's family, I learned to love her family. Her Dad, in his 80's, a retired Army Air Force pilot, a bit handicapped from the ravages of aging, and I spent many hours talking. When he passed over at the age of 93, Marcia's and my lost was deep. One morning soon after he died, I woke to see a penny sitting on the edge of the upper drawer of my dresser. There is a lip out over it—the drawer was closed tight. It glistened in the morning sun. I called Marcia's attention to it and we exclaimed it came from her Dad. I tried many, many times to place it there, but it wouldn't stay. We thanked Dad and marveled.

Now, I begin the backstretch of my life. What will it bring? How long will it be? What new will I experience?

It seems that the death of my brother, Nelson, in March of 2015, brought some reality about life and death and added some urgency to finish this book. How quickly life moves! It seems only yesterday that he and I were kids, fighting like cats and dogs, getting lickin's as a consequence, and trying to figure out this thing called sex, listening to the radio while taking a long time to wash his car, driving to church youth meetings, etc.

The last number of years, Nelson, his son, Jerry and a couple of his friends took annual trips to golf at Myrtle Beach. The discussions invoked numerous arguments, sometimes heated, about politics or religion. But, those were special times, with him—he always let down his hair with me, drank some, swore more, and groused about his life.

Life has been a rich experience for me. It has not always been kind, but I embrace that. I feel that I've been privileged to see, hear, to play, to endure more than ever expected. I still desire to have much more and intend to continue to live life to the fullest. I could not have a better person to grow old with then Marcia and I am deeply grateful. **"I did it my way"**

Two roads diverged in a yellow wood, and I—
I took the one less traveled by,
And that has made all the difference.

Vita

Dr. Carroll J. Lehman

EDUCATION
Degrees

1975	Doctor of Musical Arts in Vocal Performance and Pedagogy:
	University of Iowa
	Thesis: *Benjamin Carr: His contribution to Early American Solo Vocal Literature*
1968	Master of Arts in Vocal Music
	University of Iowa
1964	Bachelor of Science in Music Education
	Eastern Mennonite College

Private study in Voice

Rudolf Knoll	Mozarteum, Salzburg, Austria
Leon Lishner	Seattle, Washington
Hermanus Baer	Chicago, Illinois
Albert Gammon	University of Iowa

Conducting Workshops

Helmut Rilling	Oregon Bach Festival	Eugene, Oregon
Robert Shaw	Westminister Choir College	

Elmer Isler   Dartmouth Choral Workshop
Paul Salmonavich
Albert McNeil
Robert DeCormier

SABBATICALS

1998	Continued my research and study of vocal therapy. Boston: Workshops with the McCloskey Institute
	Workshops with Dr. Robert Sataloff and other clinicians
1991	New York City: 4 months of attending vocal master classes including one led by Pavarotti
	Going to many concerts and operas.
	Studied voice and vocal therapy
1984	Vocal Study in Salzburg, Austria with Rudolf Knoll Summer Academy, Mozarteum
	Continued private study from September to December

PROFESSIONAL ACTIVITIES

Teacher

1978 – 2015	Professor of Music
	Keene State College,
	Keene, New Hampshire
1975 - 1978	Voice Instructor
	Western Washington University,
	Bellington, Washington
1970 – 1975	Assistant Professor of Music
	Hope College,
	Holland, Michigan

1964 – 1966   Secondary Vocal and Choral Teacher
                   Western Mennonite School,
                   Salem, Oregon

Courses taught in colleges
    Private studio voice   Vocal pedagogy
    Class voice   Choral Literature
    Diction for singers   Conducting
    Opera workshop   Choral Methods
    Vocal Literature   Introduction to Music Masterworks

Some of the schools my students have graduated from with advanced degrees
    Boston Conservatory
    Eastman School of music
    New England Conservatory
    Julliard
    Temple University
    Florida State University
    University of Arizona
    Kansas City Conservatory
    Boston University
    University of Massachusetts, Amherst
    Shenandoah Conservatory

PROFESSIONAL AFFILIATIONS
    National Association of Teacher of Singing
        State, Regional and National Conventions
        Adjudicator on State, Regional and National Levels
        Former New Hampshire State Governor
        Winners and Finalists in Competitions
        Former member and Secretary of the Board of Boston Chapter
    American Choral Directors Association
        Past State President

Music Educators National Conference
    Still active as All –State Audition Judge
    Presented several workshops at All-State Conference
    Twice directed annual vocal chamber music festival
Music Teachers National Association
    Adjudicator in State and National Auditions

VOCAL PERFORMANCES

Selected Opera Roles

Count	Marriage of Figaro	Mozart
Dr. Bartolo		
Figaro		
Sarastro	Magic Flute (concert version)	
Guglielmo	Cosi fan tutte	
El Capitan	El Capitan	Sousa
Aeneas	Dido and Aeneas	Purcell
Simone	Gianni Schicchi	Puccini
Peachum	Beggar's Opera	Gay
Germont	La Traviata	Verdi
The Marquis		
Jupiter	Orpheus in the Underworld	Offenbach
Bert	Four Thousand Dollars	Turner
Fiorello	Barber of Seville	Rossini
Judge	Trial by Jury	Sullivan
Dr. Blind	Die Fledermaus	Strauss

Selected Oratorio Roles with orchestra

Messiah	Handel
Israel in Eygpt	
Te Deum	Kodaly
Te Deum	Bruckner
St. John's Passion	Bach
Magnificat	

Ich habe genug
C Minor Mass   Mozart
C Major Mass
Requiem
Requiem   Brahms
Fantasia on Christmas Carol   V. Williams
Five Mystical Songs
Magnificat   Vivaldi
Mass in C   Beethoven
Lord Nelson Mass   Haydn
Theresa Mass
Creation
Elijah   Mendelssohn
Solo recitals in Washington, Michigan, Pennsylvania, Virginia, Iowa and New Hampshire

Conductor and Music Director
  Keene State College
    Opera Workshop
    Oratorio Society
    Concerto/Aria Concert
    Concert Choir
    Chamber Singers,

  Works with Chorus and Orchestra
    Bach   Magnificat
    Cantata 140
    Ninth Symphony   Beethoven
    Choral Fantasy
    Requiem   Brahms
    Requiem   Fauré
    Messiah   Handel
    Creation   Haydn

"Theresa "Mass
"Lord Nelson" Mass
Requiem   Mozart
Mass in C major
Carmina Burana   Orff
Requiem   Verdi
Gloria   Vivaldi

Operas and Musicals
  Music directed and staged many scenes from operas including
  The Marriage of Figaro   Mozart
  Magic Flute
  Cosi fan tutte
  Hansel and Gretel   Humperdinck
  Carmen   Bizet
  Orfeo   Monteverdi
  Old Maid and the Thief   Menotti
  Fidelio   Beethoven

Full Productions
  Amahl and the Night Visitors   Menotti
  The Old Maid and the Thief
  Dido and Aeneas   Purcell
  Fiddler on the Roof   Bock
  Little Shop of Horrors   Menken
  Three Penny Opera   Weill

Monadnock Chorus

Works with orchestra
  Requiem   Verdi
  Elijah   Mendelssohn
  Ninth (Choral) Symphony   Beethoven

Choral Fantasia
Creation   Haydn
Seasons
"Lord Nelson" Mass
Magnificat   Bach
Christmas Oratorio
Gloria   Vivaldi
Stabat Mater   Rossini
Stabat Mater   Dvorak
Magnificat   Rutter
Requiem   Mozart
Coronation" Mass
Requiem   Brahms
Alto Rhapsody
Nanie
Carmina Burana   Orff
Mass in Ab   Schubert
Evening at the Opera
Evening of Gershwin

Themed concerts with guest conductor/clinicians
    Latin Christmas   Maria Guinand
    African American Christmas   Geoff Hicks
    Russian Christmas   Anton Belov

Conducted concert in Carnegie Hall
    April 1998 —world premiere of a commissioned work by New York
        composer, John David Earnest

International tours
    Scandinavia: Norway, Sweden, Denmark
    Greece
    Spain and Portugal

Italy, Austria, Germany
    St. Mark's Cathedral   Venice,
    St. Peter's (High Mass)   Rome
       Performed for Pope's at his weekly broadcast
    Santa Maria Fiore   Florence

New Hampshire Friendship Chorus
    International Tours:
        China
        South Africa
        Russia, Latvia, Estonia

47411279R00110

Made in the USA
Middletown, DE
24 August 2017